The Laughing Ledger

The Corporate Hustle Meets Comic Muscles.

Sanket
Agarkar

Table of Content

"My manager says we're a 'flat structure.'
That's true—so flat, I'm completely invisible."

"A purchase order is just a love letter with
terms and conditions."

"HR is like Wi-Fi. You only notice them
when something's not working."

"We don't work under pressure. We thrive in it,
bathe in it, and call it 'flexibility.'"

"If it was 'discussed,' it doesn't need to be documented.
Until someone gets blamed."

Preface

I didn't set out to write a book. I set out to survive a Monday morning meeting that could've been an email.

But somewhere between muting my mic during awkward silences and replying "Noted with thanks" through clenched teeth, I realized—I wasn't alone. We're all in this absurd, beautifully broken, caffeine-fuelled ecosystem called corporate life. And if we don't laugh at it, we might just cry... or worse, reply-all with our emotional breakdown.

The Laughing Ledger isn't a guidebook. It's not here to teach you how to climb the corporate ladder (spoiler: it's usually broken somewhere around step 3). It's a collection of moments, people, emails, and expressions you've probably seen—or sent. It's therapy in the form of sarcasm. It's every "quick sync" that turned into an existential crisis. Every "as discussed" that meant "good luck finding proof." Every smile you've faked during team-building activities involving plastic cups and broken trust.

You'll meet some familiar characters—Rajiv, the manager who never sleeps (and doesn't believe you should either). Dhaval, the overachiever who probably dreams in Excel. Sandeep, the boss's favourite with a PhD in saying "Yes, boss" before the boss even finishes the sentence. Subhash, who speaks for 80% of the meeting and says... absolutely nothing. And then there's me—the observer. Quiet, watching, sipping tea, and logging it all in my mental ledger.

This book is a mirror. Sometimes you'll laugh because it's relatable. Sometimes you'll cringe because it's *too* relatable. It's a collection of stories—of missed deadlines and miracle submissions, of HR emails that say "Your voice matters ☺" and colleagues who say "Let's align offline" when they really mean "I have no clue either."

And yes, it's funny. But it's also honest. Because behind all the madness, something strange happens—people care. Projects get done. Deadlines are (almost) met. Colleagues become allies. And once in a while, someone sends a meme in the group chat that makes the day just a little better.

So, if you've ever worked in an office (real or virtual), been part of a team, had a boss, *been* a boss, or just survived a 47-slide training module while your soul slowly left your body—this one's for you.

This is not a corporate playbook. It's a love letter to the chaos. A toast to the team meetings that never end and the coffee that never works. A gentle nudge to say—hey, it's okay. You're not the only one Googling "how to sound confident when you have no idea what's going on."

Welcome to *The Laughing Ledger*.

Keep your sarcasm sharp and your mic on mute. It's going to be a wonderfully ridiculous ride.

Dedication

To every employee who's ever typed "Please find attached" and then forgotten to attach the file—

This one's for you.

Also for the brave souls who opened a 9 p.m. email just to "check quickly."

You deserve a raise, or at least a decent cup of coffee.

Author's Note

Writing this book felt like forwarding a funny meme to every colleague I've ever worked with—except now, the meme is 200 pages long and occasionally uses bullet points.

I didn't want to write a success story. I wanted to write *our* story. The one with awkward team calls, typo-laden presentations, mysterious CCs, and oddly specific HR policies.

If, while reading, you laugh out loud and think, "Wait, this is *too* real,"—you're welcome. And I apologize.

I hope this book gives you joy, perspective, and just enough distraction during your next "quick sync" to keep your sanity intact.

Thanks for reading. Now go ahead—flip the page, sip your chai, and let's dive into the madness together.

—Sanket

"Because if we don't laugh at corporate life, we'll just end up replying-all to our breakdowns."

Let's face it—corporate life is the greatest social experiment ever conducted without ethics approval. We dress up, show up, smile in meetings we weren't supposed to be in, and nod at slides we stopped reading on Page 3. If survival of the fittest applied to workplaces, it'd be survival of the ones who mastered the mute button and pretended to take notes.

The Laughing Ledger was born somewhere between a missed deadline, a motivational quote from HR, and a budget approval that took two quarters and three VLOOKUP errors. It's not just a book—it's therapy. For all of us who've ever replied "Noted with thanks" with silent rage, or attended a team-building session that nearly broke the team.

This isn't a how-to book. It's a how-we-actually-do-it book.

We laugh at the never-ending war between managers and employees, a silent Cold War with performance reviews and Excel trackers as weapons. We laugh at HR, that mysterious tribe that appears only when it's appraisal season—or someone steals someone else's tiffin from the fridge.

We peek into the procurement zone, where "Please confirm urgently" is whispered like a prayer, and POs are sent back and forth like emotionally unavailable love letters. We look at team meetings, where one colleague talks for 45 minutes but says absolutely nothing. And somehow, that same guy volunteers to "summarize the discussion."

There are characters you'll recognize. The overenthusiastic meeting hero. The favourite of the boss. The spreadsheet ninja. The silent strategist who says one thing a week and still gets promoted. And of course, the workaholic manager whose idea of "work-life balance" is sending you messages at 1:47 AM with no subject line.

We talk about resignations, evaluations, coffee breaks, and that sacred corporate phrase: "As discussed." It has ended more friendships and saved more managers than any HR policy ever written.

But between all the chaos and caffeine, there's something beautiful. A bizarre rhythm to it all. Projects get done. Deadlines (mostly) met. People grow. Some even thrive. And once in a while, there's a genuine moment of teamwork, a pat on the back, a joke that lands just right in a meeting. Those moments? Worth holding on to.

So here's to the real heroes of corporate life: the ones who laugh through the madness, manage the madness, or quietly observe it all and turn it into a book.

Welcome to *The Laughing Ledger*. Keep your volume low and your sarcasm high. It's going to be a fun ride.

Manager Vs Employee

*"My manager says we're a 'flat structure.'
That's true—so flat, I'm completely invisible."*

Welcome to the Jungle (with Air Conditioning)

Step into any modern office, and you'll discover a jungle like no other. Not one filled with wild animals or echoing birdcalls, but a fluorescent-lit, coffee-fuelled, KPI-hunting, chaos-coordinated corporate jungle. This one comes with biometric entries, passive-aggressive email threads, and most importantly—central air conditioning. Here, survival doesn't depend on speed or strength but on your ability to survive back-to-back meetings, reply-all with diplomacy, and master the sacred art of sounding enthusiastic on Teams calls.

Welcome to a place where "ASAP" actually means "yesterday," and "Let's take it offline" means "let's never speak of this again." Where "synergy" is the battle cry, and "visibility" is the holy grail. It's a habitat where PowerPoint presentations are treated like scrolls of ancient wisdom, and the true jungle beasts are deadlines, targets, and surprise client feedback.

At the centre of this corporate wilderness is the dynamic duo: the manager and the employee. Their relationship is part chess match, part therapy session, part stand-up comedy. It's a curious dance of delegation, deliverables, and diplomatic nodding. Sometimes allies, often adversaries, they exist in a loop of unspoken expectations, annual reviews, and shared suffering over stale office snacks.

But wait—this ecosystem is richer than just two characters. It includes the overburdened boss whose to-do list grows faster than HR's policy updates. The flexible manager who's everyone's best friend until appraisal season. The chronically online workaholic who answers emails faster than you can type "Good morning." The loud meeting warrior who dominates every conversation, the boss's blue-eyed favourite who somehow "coincidentally" gets the best projects, and the silent observer—always listening, always watching, silently climbing the ladder.

Each cubicle houses a story, each Slack ping carries hidden meaning, and each "quick sync" could derail your day (or your soul).

This book is an unfiltered, witty exploration of this chaotic ecosystem—part roast, part reality check, and a whole lot of "OMG, this is too real." So, tighten your tie, adjust your posture, and brace yourself for a tour through the most unpredictable terrain ever mapped—the corporate office.

Because here in the jungle, the only thing more dangerous than deadlines... is running out of coffee.

The Laughing Ledger

Manager is the person who wants a woman to deliver 9 babies in one month.

And if she does, he wants 18 in the next month.

Sanket
AGARKAR

1. Manager vs. Employee: The Daily Cold War

No office saga is as timeless—or as silently dramatic—as the ongoing tension between a manager and their employee. Think Cold War, but with more Excel sheets and fewer missiles.

At 9:01 AM, Mr. Mehta, the ever-optimistic manager, pings his team:

Mr. Mehta: "Let's jump on a quick call?"

Rohan (internally): "There goes my will to live. Again."

As the token observer in this battlefield, I sip my coffee quietly, watching Rohan's soul exit his body via Zoom.

The relationship between Mr. Mehta and Rohan is best described as... diplomatically dysfunctional.

Rohan: "I've shared the draft version as discussed."

Mr. Mehta: "Yes, but what I meant was a detailed draft, with slides, notes, and projected outcomes."

Rohan: "So... not what we discussed."

Me: *Sips coffee louder.*

The **Struggle** is real—and universal. Rohan craves clarity, peace, and ideally, a lunch break longer than five minutes. Mr. Mehta, on the other hand, seeks accountability, ownership, and everything in Arial 11 with perfect bullet alignment.

The real tension lies in unspoken expectations: Rohan hopes his manager will magically know what he means by "WIP." Mr. Mehta hopes Rohan magically knows what he means by "deliverable."

Mr. Mehta: "I need this urgently."

Rohan: "Define urgently."

Mr. Mehta: "Before the client even thinks of it."

Rohan (muted): "So, time travel. Cool."

Each day is a tug-of-war—Rohan pulling for balance, Mr. Mehta pulling for bandwidth. And yet, like some miracle orchestrated by corporate chaos theory, the project gets delivered. Usually at 11:59 PM, after a shared moment of panic and a hundred edits later.

In this daily duel, no one truly wins—but no one quits either. Because beneath the banter, tension, and passive-aggressive calendar invites, there's grudging respect, shared suffering, and the unspoken bond forged by deadlines.

As for me? I observe, I laugh (silently), and I pray Mr. Mehta never asks me to "jump on a quick call."

The Laughing Ledger

'Flexible hours' just means you're available to work all the time."

Sanket
AGARKAR

2. The Overburdened Manager: Carrying More Than Just Pressure

There are two types of managers in every office—those who micromanage, and those who are so overwhelmed they can't remember if they had lunch... last week. Enter **Dwitesh**, our legendary Customer Care Manager, a man whose calendar is a solid block of colour and whose inbox has achieved sentience.

Swapnil: "Sir, just following up on that pending feedback from last month..."

Dwitesh: *[Looking up with glazed eyes]* "Was that from this year?"

Me: *Observing silently* — It's like watching a tired octopus try to juggle flaming swords.

Dwitesh is the kind of manager who starts a sentence, forgets it halfway, then sends a Teams message about it three days later. His to-do list is so long, it got shortlisted for a Booker Prize.

The Advantage (for employees like Swapnil):

You can miss a deadline, and Dwitesh won't notice—because he missed his own.

You can move a meeting, and he'll actually **thank you** for the breathing room.

You can ask for feedback, and what you'll get is a **5-second stare**, followed by an existential sigh that belongs in a French film.

Swapnil: "Dwitesh sir, should we escalate this issue to the client?"

Dwitesh: *[Clicking six tabs at once]* "Yes. No. Wait. What are we talking about again?"

Swapnil: "The client's email."

Dwitesh: "Right. Which client?"

Swapnil: "The one who pays us."

Dwitesh: "Ah. Yes. Escalate—but gently. Use Comic Sans."

The Downside:

Zero direction.

Approvals take longer than getting a passport during peak season.

And Swapnil? He's become an independent unit of survival—self-managed, slightly cynical, but quietly thriving under managerial invisibility.

Dwitesh, meanwhile, walks the halls with a laptop charger in hand and hope in his heart, forever chasing the mythical "clear inbox." He's less of a manager now, and more of a philosophical concept—rumoured to exist, rarely spotted, and when found, always tired.

Me (still observing): If Dwitesh were a superhero, his power would be attending five meetings at once and hearing none of them.

And somehow, despite the chaos, the department still runs. Barely. But hey—that's corporate life.

The
Laughing
Ledger

"We'll keep it short'—and then proceed to have a 2-hour meeting."

Sanket
AGARKAR

3. The Flexible Manager: The Cool Parent of Corporate Life

Every office has one: the *cool* manager. Not the one who micromanages font sizes or schedules "urgent" 7 p.m. syncs on Fridays — no, we're talking about **Varun**, the Marketing Manager with hoodie vibes and trust issues (not with people, but with upper management).

Suneeta: "Varun sir, I might need an extension on the campaign deck…"

Varun: *[Sipping oat milk latte]* "Take your time, I trust your creative process."

Me (observing silently): Translation: *He forgot there was a deadline.*

Qualities of a Flexible Manager:

Believes autonomy > authority.

Will remind you to take mental health breaks... while forgetting their own.

Thinks KPIs should come *after* chai and *before* peace of mind.

Suneeta: "The client meeting is at 4, right?"

Varun: "Technically yes, but spiritually... 4:15."

Me: I've never seen someone treat stress with so much yoga energy and so little calendar discipline.

Compromises They Make:

Flexible managers *will* cover for you. Even if that means designing the last 4 slides themselves at midnight while whispering affirmations like, "This is fine."

They fight for your leave approvals harder than you do.

They gently deflect blame like seasoned diplomats.

They say things like, "It's okay, let's learn from this," while dying inside.

Suneeta: "I forgot to send that follow-up email to the client."

Varun: "That's okay, I'll just call them and pretend it's part of our surprise engagement strategy."

Suneeta: "You're the best."

Me: *Watches as Varun opens his sixth browser tab titled "burnout symptoms."*

The Downside?

Upper management sees Varun's kindness as *inefficiency*. He's praised for team morale but punished with extra responsibilities. His team loves him — they'd walk through fire for him, but he's the one holding the extinguisher *and* the HR policy handbook.

After months of being the team's emotional shock absorber and creative safety net, Varun did the unthinkable: he took a **vacation**.

Varun (in a farewell Teams message):

"Off to the mountains for a digital detox. Please *don't* email.

Please *do* shine."

Suneeta (in the team group chat):

"OMG, it's happening. Varun left the chat."

The moment his out-of-office reply activated, the office atmosphere shifted.

Me (observing): You could hear the silence of creative panic. Also, someone brought cake to celebrate "freedom."

With Varun gone, Suneeta was unofficially in charge. She started strong — organized a team huddle, scheduled a brainstorm, even wore formal shoes.

Then came the client email.

Then came the panic.

Then came the typo in the subject line: *"Campain Launch - Plz Ignre Erorr"*

Suneeta (wide-eyed): "Should I unsend? Should I quit? Should I run away and start a candle business?"

But here's the twist. The client... **loved** it.

Client reply:

"This raw, real, anti-perfection email? Such authentic branding! Can we make this a series?"

Suneeta (to me): "WHAT?! This was not strategy. This was a typo!"

Me: "Never underestimate the power of chaos wrapped in confidence."

In 72 hours, the "Campain Series" gained unexpected traction. Engagement soared. The hashtag **#PlzIgnreErorr** trended. Even the CEO shared it with a fire emoji.

By the time Varun returned, glowing from his Himalayan retreat and suspiciously unaware of Slack updates, the team was... famous.

Varun (scrolling through his inbox):

"What on Earth happened?"

Suneeta: "We have launched an accidental campaign. And it worked."

Varun: *Stares into the void* "I leave for five days and we become viral meme lords."

Me: "You should take vacations more often."

"Sometimes, you don't need a strategy. You need a typo, a little panic, and a flexible manager on vacation."

Me (thinking): Varun is the reason employees don't quit.

Also me: Varun is the reason other managers do.

He's not just managing a team; he's managing *expectations* — his team's hopes and dreams, and his own rapidly vanishing sanity.

The
Laughing
Ledger

Manager: "Where do you see yourself in five years?"

Employee: "Not here, if these meetings keep happening."

4. The Strict Boss and His Fearfully Productive Employee

There are bosses who inspire. There are bosses who coach.

And then there's **Pratik**, the Finance Manager whose Outlook emails give heart palpitations and whose keyboard clicks sound like corporate Morse code for "you messed up."

You can feel his presence even before you see him. The air near his cabin drops a few degrees. His desk has precisely stacked files, a calculator with trust issues, and a paperweight shaped like a disappointed auditor.

Pratik (on Teams): "Need report. Today."

Joyce (reading): "Was that a request or a prophecy?"

As a silent observer (me), I've watched **Joyce**, his eternally anxious yet supremely productive direct report, evolve from enthusiastic executive to caffeinated spreadsheet ninja.

Joyce (at 8:03 AM):

"Just finished Pratik's Q3 projection deck."

Me: "Weren't we in Q2?"

Joyce: "He believes in being ahead of stress."

She doesn't wait for feedback—she builds contingency decks *just in case*. I once saw her finish a presentation *before* she was assigned to it.

Pratik: "We need to revise our YoY growth assumptions."

Joyce: "Done. And I've created 3 backup models, 2 graphs, and an emotional support pie chart."

Her success is powered by fear, perfectionism, and 3 cups of espresso before 10 AM. She's also memorized Pratik's breathing patterns, which she swears helps her time when to submit files.

The kicker? Pratik doesn't raise his voice. He doesn't micromanage. **He simply exists**—like gravity, and just as heavy.

Joyce (at lunch): "Sometimes I dream in Excel."

Me: "That's... unhealthy."

Joyce: "But my formulas are flawless."

Pratik might never give a standing ovation, or even a smile, but when he mutters, *"good work"*, it echoes like thunder on a dry day. Joyce once took the rest of the day off after hearing that.

The Laughing Ledger

Manager: "What's your plan for today?"

Employee: "To make it through without quitting."

5. Who's Who in the Zoo: The Office Cast

Welcome to the wild, chaotic zoo we call the workplace. If you observe long enough (as I often do while pretending to adjust PowerPoint margins), you'll notice patterns. And people. And recurring characters who seem straight out of a corporate soap opera, just with more emails and fewer ad breaks.

Let me introduce you to our elite cast:

1. Rajiv – The Workaholic Supply Chain Manager

He doesn't sleep. He syncs with spreadsheets.

Rajiv (at 3:01 AM): "Gentle reminder – please share Q3 procurement tracker."

Me (in my dreams): "Gentle reminder – please sleep."

Dhaval (grudgingly): "Replying with one eye open."

Rajiv considers weekends as "non-working full workdays."

2. Dhaval – The One Super Performer

Dhaval, the Supply Chain Executive, delivers results faster than the delivery apps he negotiates with.

Manager (in review): "You've done the work of 4 people."

Dhaval: "Can I get the salary of even 1.5?"

Team (collectively): *glares in underperformance*

Dhaval's biggest enemies? Unrealistic deadlines. And his jealous colleagues.

3. Sandeep – Rajiv's Favourite

Sandeep works in Data Centre Logistics and possesses the rare immunity of being untouchable.

Rajiv: "He's got potential."

Me: "He's also got a 4-hour lunch break."

Everyone else: *debating if "potential" is a skill*

He once crashed a server and was rewarded with a coffee voucher. We crash an Excel file, and it's an HR-level incident.

4. Subhash – The Hyperactive Meeting Champ

Subhash has a KPI: **Talk for 80% of the meeting time.** Contribution: Pending.

Subhash: "Let me add a few points."

Everyone (internally): "Brace for verbal marathon."

Me: *counts ceiling tiles until it's over*

He starts sentences with "Let's ideate" and ends with "...you know what I mean." We rarely do.

5. Me – The Observer

I watch. I listen. I note. I mute.

Colleague: "Why don't you say much?"

Me: "Because I like my job… and drama-free Fridays."

But when I do speak in meetings? Slack lights up. Screenshots are taken. Eyes widen. It's like watching a unicorn give a TED Talk.

Each of these characters plays their part in the grand production. Some drive results. Some drive us mad. But together? They make Monday mornings *just* tolerable enough.

6. Two Reporting Managers: The Ultimate Workplace Curse

If having one boss is a full-time job, having two is a divine punishment wrapped in Outlook invites.

Meet Santosh — Operations Executive and unwilling protagonist of this corporate custody drama. He reports to *Manish* from Product and *Junaid* from Sales. I, as always, sit quietly nearby, sipping my chai and watching his soul slowly evacuate his body via Teams notifications.

Monday, 10:00 AM

Manish: "Santosh, I need you to finalize the product deck by EOD."

Junaid (simultaneously): "Santosh, update the sales tracker first. It's urgent!"

Santosh: "Should I clone myself or just flip a coin?"

The best part? Both managers use phrases like "this shouldn't take long" for tasks that could power an MBA course.

Tuesday, 3:00 PM

Manish: "Did you get my email?"

Santosh: "Which one?"

Manish: "The one I marked 'URGENT', 'RESPONSE NEEDED', and 'CONFIDENTIAL'."

Santosh: "Ah yes, it was buried under Junaid's 'IMMEDIATE ACTION REQUIRED', 'PRIORITY' and 'TOP LEVEL' tags."

Me (silently): "How does his inbox survive this?"

The *real* magic begins during performance reviews.

Manish: "He's good, but reactive."

Junaid: "He's proactive, but needs direction."

HR (confused): "So... he's Schrodinger's employee?"

Side Effects of Dual Reporting:

Conflicting priorities: One says focus on long-term strategy, the other wants daily updates.

Double the calls: And they both think "quick sync" means *45 minutes of trauma.*

Diluted clarity: Your job description becomes, essentially, "whatever they don't agree on."

Santosh has learned to survive using ancient diplomatic arts — vague replies, expert-level calendar blocking, and the occasional "lost in transit" excuse for emails.

Santosh: "I thought you were aligned on that task?"

Manish & Junaid (together): "We never discussed it."

Me (drily): "Can we align on who's misaligned?"

By Friday, Santosh looks like he's aged three fiscal quarters. But he soldiers on. Because in the end, having two bosses means double the stress... but also double the chances to dodge accountability.

Now if only he could get them to CC each other instead of him on everything.

7. The Workaholic Manager and the Clock-Watching Team

You met Rajiv, right? Our legendary Supply Chain Manager who thinks sleep is for the weak and weekends are for reviewing spreadsheets. While most managers have office hours, Rajiv has office seconds—because he's online. Always. Somewhere between "Good Morning" and "It's 2 AM, sir," lies his comfort zone.

As I sip my 4 PM chai quietly, Rajiv bursts in:

Rajiv: "Team, we've got a critical client update. Let's jump on a quick sync at 9 PM."

Team (in sync): "Uhh... Sir, that's family time..."

Rajiv: "Exactly! And nothing builds stronger work-family relations than syncing with your *work* family."

Swapnil, clock-watching executive, mutters in the group chat, "I didn't sign up to be adopted by Rajiv sir."

The team has developed survival instincts.

Harsh sets his Slack to "Offline" every evening but keeps one eye open.

Priya fakes network issues during post-dinner calls.

Vishal claims his cat sits on his keyboard after 8 PM. Every day.

Rajiv, however, is relentless. His laptop battery has died fewer times than he has blinked in a day.

Rajiv (11:45 PM email): "Just one thought before I sleep—can we realign our targets?"

Team (group chat): "He sleeps?!?"

Yet, strangely, work gets done. Rajiv's urgency infects the team with last-minute panic energy that somehow meets every deadline. But the cost?

I've watched this dynamic evolve like a slow-burn series. Rajiv's fire never dims. But the team? They've started wearing blue-light glasses, not for eye strain—but to hide the tears.

Still, there's an odd respect. As much as they grumble, they deliver. Because somewhere, deep beneath the caffeine haze and late-night madness, Rajiv does push them to grow. Exhausted? Yes. Overwhelmed? Definitely. But better? Marginally.

Just don't call a meeting past 7 PM. That's when the memes start flying.

"Rajiv doesn't believe in work-life balance. He believes in work-life fusion—with extra deadlines."

8: The Super Performer vs. The Jealous Colleagues

Every office has a Dhaval. The unicorn of output, the spreadsheet sorcerer, the one who delivers before the deadline and still manages to correct your grammar in the team email.

Rajiv, the supply chain manager, glows every time Dhaval's name is mentioned in townhalls. You can practically see a tear forming in his left eye—out of pride, or maybe exhaustion from micro-managing everyone *except* Dhaval.

Rajiv: "Team, let's all try to match Dhaval's dedication."

Jealous Colleague 1 (muttering): "What's next? A Dhaval statue?"

Jealous Colleague 2: "Maybe we should rename the group 'Team Dhaval featuring Others'."

I, the silent observer, sip my chai and nod. It's showtime again.

Dhaval: "I just shared a draft of the inventory projection till Q4."

Jealous Colleague 3: "Of course you did, Dhaval. Did you also solve world hunger on your coffee break?"

While Dhaval powers through deliverables like a human ERP system, the rest are busy launching passive-aggressive memes on the WhatsApp group titled "Not All Heroes Wear Headsets."

Rajiv: "Excellent job, Dhaval. Your work ethic is an example for all."

Dhaval: "Thanks, sir. Just trying to help."

Colleague (under breath): "And raise the bar so high we need a forklift."

To be fair, super performers like Dhaval carry the load when others are off 'synergizing' in pointless meetings. But office dynamics are rarely fair.

Some want to be him. Some want to dethrone him. Most just want him to take a vacation so they can breathe.

As for me? I've learned to quietly observe, clap politely, and forward Dhaval's tracker as my own when no one's looking.

Teams need a Dhaval to run, and jealous colleagues to provide the entertainment.

"Team player: someone who works hard so the team can take credit (and gossip)."

9. The Boss's Favourite: Corporate Royalty

Every workplace has one. The chosen one. The golden child. The Boss's Favourite. In our office, that role is played flawlessly by *Sandeep*, who seems to have unlocked the cheat codes to corporate survival.

While the rest of us fumble through spreadsheets and performance reviews, Sandeep glides. Literally. He has a chair that doesn't creak. An aura that smells faintly of approval. And a passcode to Rajiv's good books.

One Monday morning, Rajiv walks in. I sip coffee quietly in the corner.

Rajiv: "Any thoughts on the new inventory process?"

Dhaval: "Yes, I've compiled a full report with—"

Rajiv: "Let's hear from Sandeep first."

Sandeep: (opens mouth slowly) "Maybe we can automate… something?"

Rajiv: "Brilliant! That's the kind of innovative thinking I want!"

Dhaval: (whispers) "That *was* my idea."

Me (observing silently): I saw that coming. So did Dhaval's blood pressure.

Sandeep's real skill isn't in operations. It's in alignment — with Rajiv's mood, tone, and font preferences. His most used phrase? "Yes, boss." His second most used? "Love that idea, boss."

We once heard him say "No" — but only to a cookie during his diet phase. Never to Rajiv.

He sits front row in meetings, laughs two seconds earlier than anyone else at Rajiv's jokes, and has mastered the humble brag. "I just happened to stay till 11 PM yesterday... nothing major."

His desk? Next to Rajiv's cabin. His email replies? Start with "As discussed with Rajiv..." whether or not Rajiv was ever involved.

Rajiv: "Sandeep, any challenges you're facing?"

Sandeep: "Only that I can't work more than 18 hours a day, boss."

Rajiv: (laughs) "Now that's commitment!"

Me (mentally): Or Stockholm Syndrome.

But here's the twist. While favouritism might irk us mere mortals, Sandeep's role serves a purpose. He's the buffer. The yes-man who absorbs Rajiv's wildest ideas before they reach the rest of us. A shield of flattery that protects us from sudden "restructuring" plans.

So, while we pretend to grumble, deep down we're relieved. Let him reign.

Long live the Favourite.

"It's not what you know, it's who you laugh at the boss's jokes with."

10. The Hyperactive Meeting Hero

Every office has one. That employee who doesn't just attend meetings — they *own* them. Enter **Subhash**, our resident meeting marathoner. He doesn't walk into rooms — he *enters stages*. His voice? Always set to "project." His slides? Endless. His contribution? Questionable.

I've often joked (silently, to myself of course) that if there were an Olympic event for "Most Words Spoken Without Meaning," Subhash would have multiple golds... and a PowerPoint about it.

One Monday Morning Sync. I sip coffee. Everyone's screens are off. Except one.

Rajiv (Manager): "Any quick updates before we dive in?"

Subhash (already unmuted): "Yes, Rajiv. Let me quickly walk you through a 14-slide deck I made over the weekend. Title: *Strategic Synergy for Cross-Functional Visibility in Q2.*"

Dhaval (muted): "We just wanted a status update."

Sandeep (smiling): "Brilliant title, Subhash!"

Me (internally): This better come with popcorn.

Subhash begins with a quote from Steve Jobs, throws in some pie charts that don't quite match the data, and says "Let me build on that" every time someone else speaks. Even if the original point was about cafeteria timings.

He once "took the lead" on a brainstorming session. He spoke for 40 minutes. We brainstormed ways to make him stop.

Rajiv: "Subhash, these are… quite comprehensive slides. But do we have the latest delivery numbers?"

Subhash: "Absolutely. Slide 32. But before that, let me take you through this concept I call 'Proactive Silence.' It's where we *choose* not to speak… strategically."

Joyce (in chat): "Is that what we've been doing while he talks?"

Strangely, though Subhash rarely finishes tasks, he's always *there* — popping into calls, nodding furiously, and using words like "synergy," "pipeline," and "let's action that." We've considered making a bingo card.

And yet… his enthusiasm? Infectious. His energy? Undeniable. In a world of cameras off and mics muted, Subhash shows up.

Loudly. Visibly. Sometimes unnecessarily.

But he reminds us of something important — that visibility sometimes *is* a skill. Even if substance hasn't RSVP'd yet.

So we let him build on things. Just not our tasks.

"Some people work. Others just 'circle back' in meetings."

11. The Silent Strategist: Master of the Game

Every office has a Subhash. Loud, energetic, everywhere.

But every office *needs* a Silent Strategist — the quiet mastermind who rarely speaks, but when they do… meetings pause, coffees tremble, and even Rajiv stops mid-sentence.

Hi. That's me.

While my colleagues are busy out-synergizing each other in meetings or fighting over who sent the last email thread (with "Urgent!!" in the subject line), I watch. I listen. I plot.

My face reveals nothing. My mind is a mental Kanban board with post-its of power.

One day of Monthly review, Rajiv in full command mode. Subhash already 12 slides in. I, quietly sipping tea.

Rajiv (Manager): "Okay, I think Subhash covered the major important points. Any suggestions?"

Subhash: "I think we should proactively pivot our deliverables into a KPI-first approach aligned with our objectives"

Me: "Why not just fix the inventory filter issue first? That's why our lead times spiked."

Pause. Long silence. Subhash slowly minimizes his deck.

Rajiv: "…That's a great point. Can we get that sorted by EOD?"

Me (nods): "Already fixed it. Just needed access approval last week."

You see, I don't shout my wins. I let the results speak, whispering sweet success into Rajiv's KPI dreams.

My strategy is simple:

Attend all meetings. Speak in only one.

Avoid drama. Observe *who* creates it and *who* benefits.

Never volunteer. But always deliver.

That's how I got tagged for a leadership program without saying a word. The loud ones clapped for me while I quietly accepted.

With a smile and a mysterious "Thanks."

Rajiv: "You never say much, do you?"

Me: "Words are expensive. I invest wisely."

Rajiv (laughing): "You're dangerous."

Me (smiling): "Only when needed."

The Silent Strategist doesn't need the spotlight.

We *are* the spotlight — just set on a timer.

And by the time others realize it... we've already won the game, left the Zoom call, and updated the tracker.

"Speak softly, but carry a killer spreadsheet."

Roles, Rants, and Realizations

If corporate life had a soundtrack, it would be the gentle hum of fluorescent lights interrupted by someone whispering, *"Can everyone see my screen?"*

In the grand theatre of office drama, the roles of manager and employee are often mistaken for opposing forces. One leads. One follows. One delegates. The other dodges.

But here's the truth: it's less about hierarchy and more about harmony (or the glorious lack of it).

The Laughing Ledger

"Managers: 'Take ownership of this project!'—Translation: 'When it fails, it's your fault.'"

Sanket AGARKAR

Rajiv (Manager): "This is a vision-driven exercise."

Me (thinking): "Sir, we're designing a purchase order template."

Rohan (Employee): "Should I add the column you asked for last week?"

Rajiv: "I've had a change in vision."

Managers bring alignment, strategy, and weekly doses of ambiguity. They attend meetings to decide the date of the next meeting. They say things like "Let's circle back" and "It's not urgent, but I need it in an hour."

Employees, on the other hand, are the fuel. We execute, innovate, grumble in muted calls, and secretly build better versions of everything—because the manager's version "just needs polishing." With a flamethrower.

But here's the wild part—when both roles *actually* sync, something magical happens:

Decks get built without losing souls.

Clients are impressed (and sometimes awake).

Emails are clear. Deadlines are met.

The printer works. (Okay, maybe not that magical.)

Sandeep (Boss's Favourite): "I've aligned with Rajiv on this deck."

Dhaval (Super Performer): "I rebuilt it last night."

Subhash (Meeting Hero): "Let me build on that..."

Me: *quietly sends final version to client*

The realization? Everyone has a part to play. The manager's job is to give direction—even if it's occasionally from a moving car. The employee's job is to deliver—even if it means ignoring three conflicting instructions and just doing what's right.

And when it all works, someone finally says:

Rajiv: "Let's close the loop."

Peace... until the next loop begins. Probably with, "Quick sync?" at 8:59 AM. Because in corporate life, realization is fleeting. But the rants? Eternal.

"Between KPIs and chai breaks, harmony hides."

Supplier and Buyer

"A purchase order is just a love letter with terms and conditions."

In the grand theatre of corporate life, no relationship is quite as hilariously complicated—or suspiciously co-dependent—as that between suppliers and buyers. It's not just about transactions and terms. It's about trust, drama, delayed deliveries, and passive-aggressive emails.

Think of it like an arranged marriage: both parties are introduced by procurement, forced to work together, pretend to get along in meetings, and somehow make the relationship function without throwing purchase orders at each other. The supplier always claims, "We can deliver in 5 working days," which in supplier language means: "We'll ghost you for 4 and show up on the 5th with half the shipment and full confidence." The buyer, on the other hand, is known to demand discounts the way aunties ask for wedding snacks—loudly, repeatedly, and with no shame.

At the heart of this tango lies the holy grail: the Purchase Order (PO). It's essentially a corporate love letter—but one that includes payment terms, penalties, and footnotes about GST. A PO represents commitment. And if the supplier misses that commitment? Well, welcome to Excel-fuelled rage and four-hour status calls.

This relationship is peppered with classic one-liners:

Buyer: "Please confirm urgently."

Supplier: "Noted. Checking with the team." (Translation: They haven't even opened the email.)

Buyer: "Can we expedite this?"

Supplier: "We're already on priority." (Spoiler: You are not.)

But it's not all chaos. When the chemistry is right—when the buyer gives clarity and the supplier delivers on time—it's a match made in procurement heaven. Coffee is shared. Feedback is exchanged. And both parties feel like they're winning.

Yet, this rare harmony is often short-lived. Because the next order is already delayed, and someone forgot to attach the invoice.

In the coming sub-chapters, we'll explore every hilarious, frustrating, and painfully relatable phase of this corporate courtship— from awkward introductions and missed deliveries to rekindled partnerships and discounts disguised as apologies.

Fasten your seatbelts and keep your PO handy. This is going to be a beautifully chaotic ride through the world of Supplier & Buyer.

The Laughing Ledger

Supplier: "We pride ourselves on customer satisfaction."

Buyer: "Great! Now satisfy me with a lower price!"

Sanket
AGARKAR

1: The Courtship – RFPs and RFQs

"Swiping right on corporate compatibility."

Every great corporate love story begins with a little formal flirtation. In the supplier-buyer world, it comes in the form of RFPs (Request for Proposals) and RFQs (Request for Quotations). This is essentially the "Hi, we're available. Are you?" phase of the relationship. Like a very stiff, Excel-powered version of Tinder.

Enter **Sandeep**, the Supply Chain Manager's favorite at our company. Suave, well-dressed, and fluent in "procurementese." And then there's **Roshan**, the overly confident Sales Manager from the supplier side. Roshan walks into every meeting as if he's already won the deal—and Sandeep's admiration.

I, as usual, sat in the background with my notebook, pretending to take notes but mostly live-commenting the drama in my head.

Sandeep: "We're looking for partners, not just vendors."

Roshan: "Absolutely! We don't supply materials—we build legacies."

Me (thinking): He also once sent cement to a company that ordered sand.

The courtship begins with the buyer sending out an RFP, which is a 47-page document that no one has time to read. The supplier responds with an RFQ that's equally long and includes several references to "competitive pricing" and "quality assurance," both of which will be questioned in the very first delivery.

Roshan: "We're offering an exclusive rate. Just for you."

Sandeep: "Exclusive? You sent the same quote to our competitors. I saw the CC."

Roshan (laughs nervously): "We believe in transparency."

Me (internally): And copy-paste.

This phase is all about sizing each other up. Sandeep wants reliability. Roshan wants the PO. Both will smile, nod, and schedule the "next round of discussions" that could've been an email.

Somewhere in this carefully choreographed ritual lies the unspoken hope: that this relationship won't end in a missed dispatch or a rejected GRN (Goods Receipt Note).

It's a dance. A game. A spreadsheet-fueled romance where the first impression isn't made with flowers, but with proper documentation, on-time samples, and an Excel file that doesn't crash.

This is just the beginning. If this courtship works, we move on to the engagement: negotiations. And trust me, that's where the drama really begins.

2:   The First Date – Initial Meetings

"Where optimism meets Outlook invites."

Ah, the first meeting — the corporate equivalent of a first date. Everyone's on their best behaviour, dressed sharply, and armed with PowerPoint decks instead of flowers. It's not about love at first sight—it's about trust at first slide.

Sandeep, our Supply Chain Manager's favorite, walked into the meeting room like he was hosting a TED Talk. Across the table sat **Roshan,** the Sales Manager from the supplier company, beaming with overconfidence and one too many animations in his presentation.

I sat in the corner, pretending to take notes while actually observing body language and silently awarding points for each unnecessary acronym dropped.

Roshan (clicks to Slide 2): "At YourEx Supplies, we believe in value-driven synergy across verticals."

Sandeep (nodding): "Interesting... can you elaborate?"

Roshan (clearly stalling): "Of course! It's about aligning our core deliverables with your... um... logistical bandwidth."

Me (in my head): Translation: "We'll deliver when we can."

The energy in the room was pure hope. Roshan showed graphs that went up dramatically—probably based on nothing. Sandeep kept a straight face, nodding at every buzzword like he was trying to win "Corporate Bingo."

Sandeep: "What about lead times?"

Roshan (scrolling past that slide quickly): "Let's talk about our vision first."

Me: Lead times are like exes—everyone has them, no one wants to talk about them.

This meeting wasn't about facts. It was about vibes, optimism, and hiding red flags beneath polished language. Roshan conveniently skipped the slide about late deliveries, while Sandeep tactfully avoided asking about pricing inconsistencies... for now.

Roshan: "We see this as a long-term partnership."

Sandeep (with a diplomatic smile): "Let's start with a trial order."

Me (thinking): That's business speak for: "Let's not get ahead of ourselves."

There were smiles, handshakes, and a promise to "circle back." No one brought up the awkward quote mismatch from the RFP stage. The awkwardness of that slide font? Ignored. The coffee served during the meeting? Undrinkable. But the hope? High.

As the meeting ended, everyone walked out feeling cautiously optimistic. Like a first date that didn't go terribly wrong. Yet everyone knew—the real test would be the first delivery. Because after the first date, comes the reality check.

And Roshan had just promised 7-day delivery for materials he hadn't even procured yet.

The
Laughing
Ledger

Supplier: "The goods are with the transporter."

Buyer: "Great! Now let's hope they arrive before the next fiscal year!"

3:   The Honeymoon Phase – First Orders

"Love is blind. Especially to clause 14.3 of the terms & conditions."

After the courtship of RFPs and the hopeful first meeting, we entered the corporate version of the honeymoon phase—when everything looks shiny, polite, and dangerously perfect.

The first order was in. The PO was sent, acknowledged, and processed faster than anyone had expected. Sandeep, still glowing from the successful meeting with Roshan, strutted around the office like he'd discovered a hidden level in Excel.

Roshan (on call): "Hey Sandeep, just confirming dispatch. It's already on the truck. Left five minutes ago."

Sandeep (grinning): "On time and without me chasing you? Is this real or a simulation?"

Me (quietly sipping coffee): "Definitely a simulation. Or black magic."

Everyone was playing nice. Roshan replied to emails within minutes, and even used bullet points. Sandeep complimented Roshan on his "proactive alignment with supply milestones" (which, in normal language, means "thanks for not screwing it up").

Roshan: "We've also sent the test certificates. Page 6 has the specs you asked for."

Sandeep: "You read my mind."

Me (thinking): "Or your last five reminder emails."

Even the invoice matched the PO exactly—no rounding-off drama, no surprise line items like "logistics facilitation charge" or "documentation karma fee." It was corporate bliss.

The two of them became the poster boys of supply chain harmony. Other vendors looked on in awe, whispering things like, "Did you hear Roshan delivered on time... twice?" It was the kind of early relationship magic where both sides tried *really* hard because no one wanted to be the first to mess it up.

Sandeep even went as far as to mention Roshan's name in the internal Monday morning team call.

Sandeep (smiling in the call): "Let's all take a page from Roshan's book. Clear, timely, professional."

Me (muttering): "Wait till Chapter 4: 'The Delays Strike Back.'"

This phase is short-lived, of course. It's the calm before the shipment full of mismatched barcodes or the invoice that arrives in Comic Sans. But for now, it was perfect.

Emails were read. Deliveries were early. People used phrases like "seamless coordination" without sarcasm. And for a fleeting moment, in the land of supply and demand, everything was in balance.

But as every corporate relationship teaches us—honeymoons end. And the real marriage begins with the first stock discrepancy.

4: The First Argument – Delivery Delays

"Nothing tests love like a late delivery and a silent phone."

Just when everything seemed picture-perfect in the supplier-buyer romance, reality arrived — late, obviously.

It began with a missing consignment. The truck carrying the crucial batch of materials was supposed to arrive on Tuesday morning. It was now Thursday. Still no truck. Still no materials. Still no explanation.

Me (watching this unfold with popcorn-level interest): "And so ends the honeymoon."

Sandeep, the ever-dedicated Supply Chain Manager's favourite, had sent two polite emails, one stern follow-up, and was now preparing to unleash his signature move — the "calling-without-warning" strategy.

Sandeep (on call): "Roshan, where's the delivery? We've got production lined up and the plant manager breathing down my neck like an unpaid ghost."

Roshan (sounding too calm): "Hey buddy, there was a minor hiccup."

Sandeep: "Hiccup? You make it sound like logistics just sneezed and forgot the route!"

Roshan: "There was a supply chain disruption. The ERP system glitched."

Sandeep: "So... the system glitched, and the truck forgot how to drive?"

Roshan: "Technically, the truck was fine. The driver went home after his shift ended."

Sandeep: "Why? Was he also on a supply chain break?"

Me (internally): "Roshan better throw in a discount or a gift hamper. Or both."

The tension escalated from "cordial misunderstanding" to "Excel-attachment warfare." Sandeep forwarded the original PO, delivery schedule, and three-month-old WhatsApp screenshots. Roshan replied with GPS tracking, weather reports, and the driver's leave application. At one point, someone used the phrase, "as per our last conversation," which is basically corporate for "I'm about to lose it."

Roshan: "We value our relationship. Let's not let one delay sour things."

Sandeep: "You're right. But if this happens again, I'll be valuing a new supplier."

Roshan (softly): "Noted… very loudly."

By the end of the call, egos were bruised, patience was tested, and delivery was "promised" to arrive in the next 24 hours — corporate code for "we hope no one checks until Monday."

As I watched Sandeep fume silently and Roshan sweat through his screen, I realized: this wasn't just procurement. This was drama, diplomacy, and just the right dose of absurdity.

Ah, love in the time of logistics.

The Laughing Ledger

"Negotiation: Where both sides walk away pretending they got the better deal—but only one side truly did."

Sanket
AGARKAR

5: The Make-Up – Discount Negotiations

"Forgiveness is easier to offer when there's a 7% discount involved."

After the rocky patch — where Roshan's shipment arrived with 80% material, 20% mystery — tempers flared, calls were missed, and emails gained a suspicious number of capital letters. Tension was so thick, even the CC'd team members were sweating.

Enter: the reconciliation phase. Also known in corporate circles as "discount negotiations."

Sandeep, known for his sharp memory and sharper negotiation skills, walked into the meeting room like a man on a mission. Roshan joined virtually — with his background blurred and stress visible in 1080p.

Sandeep: "So, Roshan… about that short supply and the invoice mismatch."

Roshan: "Ah yes. The 'slight' discrepancy. Look, things got out of hand, but we're offering a gesture of goodwill…"

Sandeep (raising an eyebrow): "Please don't say coffee mugs with your logo again."

Roshan (nervous chuckle): "No mugs this time. A flat 5% discount on the next order."

Me (typing in my notepad): "Ah, the corporate version of flowers and chocolates."

Sandeep leaned back like a poker player with the upper hand. He didn't speak immediately — just let the awkward silence multiply until Roshan began to sweat like a July dispatch clerk.

Sandeep: "Hmm. 5% is cute. But so was the Excel error that cost us a client call."

Roshan: "Okay, okay. Final offer — 7% off and free freight this cycle."

Sandeep: "Add priority dispatch, and we'll pretend last week didn't happen."

Roshan: "Deal. And… no performance rating feedback this month?"

Sandeep (smirking): "Let's not get ahead of ourselves."

It was a masterclass in mutual manipulation — performed with smiles, faux humility, and Excel sheets that no one really checked.

In truth, both sides were getting what they wanted. Roshan salvaged the relationship and kept the account alive. Sandeep got the discount and the sweet satisfaction of corporate vengeance — wrapped in professionalism.

As the call ended, both men nodded respectfully, like samurais sheathing their swords.

Roshan: "Always a pleasure doing business with you, Sandeep."

Sandeep: "Let's try not doing business like last week again."

Me (to myself): "Ah, love is sweeter the second time… especially at 7% off."

In corporate life, apologies don't come in words. They come in percentages.

The Laughing Ledger

Purchase Manager: "We need a better discount."

Sales Manager: "If I give you a bigger discount, my boss will 'discount' my job!"

6:   The Seven-Year Itch – Contract Renewals

"Every long-term relationship needs a renewal… or a reality check."

Like any relationship that's been around for a while, there comes a time when both sides sit down to ask the ultimate question: "Is this still working for us?" And in the supplier-buyer world, that moment is called **contract renewal**.

Sandeep, our supply chain hero (and Rajiv's golden boy), had started dropping subtle hints that the contract with Roshan's company was up for review. Roshan, the ever-charismatic sales guy, pretended not to sweat. But oh, he was sweating.

Sandeep (smirking during a call): "So, Roshan, the contract ends next month. Just thought I'd mention it casually... like how you casually mentioned those delivery delays."

Roshan (forced laugh): "Haha, yes yes, contracts end, but partnerships? Those are eternal."

Sandeep: "Well, our procurement team is... evaluating options."

Roshan: "Evaluating? Like comparing us to... *other* vendors? That's offensive. I send you Diwali gifts, man."

Sandeep: "And we re-gifted them to Finance. It's the thought that counts."

I watched from the sidelines, sipping my tea, enjoying this episode of *Corporate Koffee with Karan*.

The negotiation meetings began. Slide decks were prepared. Cost-benefit analyses were hurled like frisbees. Roshan's team promised "enhanced service levels," "dedicated support," and "AI-powered dashboards." Sandeep's team nodded with the enthusiasm of someone watching a buffering webinar.

Sandeep: "So what's new in your offer?"

Roshan: "We've added a loyalty program."

Sandeep: "What are we, frequent flyers?"

Roshan: "You get reward points."

Sandeep: "Can I redeem them for punctual deliveries?"

By now, Roshan knew the game. He offered a revised price list, threw in a couple of performance-based clauses, and invited

Sandeep to an "off-site dinner discussion" — which Sandeep politely declined citing "Excel deadlines."

After weeks of passive-aggressive email threads, strategic silences, and "we're evaluating internally" responses, the contract was renewed. Same vendor. Slightly better terms. A new timeline for the next round of drama.

And me? Still observing. Still entertained.

Ah, the itch was scratched — for now. But in procurement love stories, there's always another clause coming.

The Laughing Ledger

Buyer: "How fast can you deliver?"

Supplier: "Depends—are we talking your timeline or reality?"

7:   The Breakup – Termination of Services

"It's not you... it's procurement."

Every relationship has its endgame. In the supplier-buyer world, that means *termination of services*. Or as Roshan liked to call it: "corporate ghosting — but with legal backing."

It began with an unusually formal email from Sandeep to Roshan. No emojis. No "bro." Just bullet points and a bolded "Effective Immediately."

Sandeep:

Dear Roshan,

After internal review, we have decided to discontinue our partnership with YourEx Supplies, effective next month. We appreciate your support thus far.

Roshan (calling immediately): "Sandeep, what's this email? You're breaking up with me over *Outlook*?"

Sandeep (calmly): "We're not breaking up, Roshan. We're professionally transitioning."

Roshan: "You sound like my ex."

Sandeep: "She sounds wise."

I sat silently in the conference room, pretending to work, while eavesdropping like a seasoned soap opera addict.

The next few days were a bureaucratic dance of detangling the relationship. Accesses were revoked. Dashboards were dismantled. Shared Excel sheets were solemnly renamed: *Final_ Report_DO_NOT_TOUCH_v12_FINAL_FINAL.xlsx.*

Roshan: "You're replacing us with that new vendor, right? I saw them on your vendor onboarding list!"

Sandeep: "No comment."

Roshan: "At least admit they'll never send memes with their quotes like I did."

Sandeep: "You once sent a Minion GIF with a credit note, Roshan. That's not exactly professionalism."

Roshan: "It got a reply, didn't it?"

They both laughed, briefly. A flicker of nostalgia. But business is business. The calls became less frequent. The chats became polite. And eventually, Roshan was removed from the vendor WhatsApp group titled *"Procure Bros ✌️ 📦."*

On the final day, a courier arrived with a box of leftover product samples and a note:

"For old time's sake. PS: Please forward any RFPs you may receive accidentally."

I watched as Sandeep looked at the box for a second longer than necessary. He didn't say much.

That's the thing with corporate breakups — there's no closure, just offboarding checklists and a final "Kind Regards."

And so, the vendor love story ended. Not with a bang, but with a formal sign-off.

The
Laughing
Ledger

"Negotiation: Crying baby gets more Milk"

8: The Rebound – New Supplier Onboarding

"Because nothing heals procurement heartbreak like a shiny new vendor presentation."

Breakups in supply chain are brutal, yes — but rebounds? Oh, they're dazzling. Enter **Hariharan**, the sharply dressed Sales Manager from **MyEx Corporation**, confidently walking into the boardroom like he was auditioning for *Shark Tank*.

Sandeep, still nursing the emotional debris from his Roshan days, was determined to keep it professional. I, your silent observer, adjusted my chair for prime eavesdropping.

Hariharan (grinning): "Sandeep-ji, we are thrilled to partner with you. At MyEx Corporation, we believe in three things — trust, timelines, and transparency."

Sandeep (under his breath): "Wow, alliteration. Very supplier-core."

Hariharan (ignoring it): "Here's our onboarding deck. It's 42 slides, but only 38 have text."

Sandeep: "That's... comforting."

Slide after slide, Hariharan dazzled with delivery metrics, photos of spotless warehouses, and one oddly dramatic testimonial from a client in Norway.

Hariharan: "We promise 100% SLA adherence."

Sandeep (raising an eyebrow): "Even during monsoons, audits, and when the boss randomly changes specs?"

Hariharan (smiling): "Especially then."

The charm offensive was real. There were branded pens, a free sample kit, and even a bar chart titled *"How We're Not Like Your Ex-Supplier."*

Sandeep (dryly): "Very subtle, Hariharan."

Hariharan: "We believe in emotional supply chain healing."

Meanwhile, Roshan's old login was deactivated, and the vendor portal got a flashy new profile: "MyExCorp_Official." I caught Sandeep hesitating before deleting Roshan's name from the Preferred Supplier tab — a silent farewell.

Back in the meeting room, Hariharan brought out a tray of cupcakes. Actual cupcakes. Branded, of course.

Hariharan: "We sweeten deals — literally."

Sandeep: "Just so you know, our last supplier once gave me a Diwali hamper with a Bluetooth speaker. You've got competition."

Hariharan (smirking): "Our Diwali kit comes with Bluetooth *and* bonus discounts."

The onboarding went smoothly. Too smoothly. Like the beginning of every relationship — full of hope, spreadsheets, and high expectations.

As I watched the two shake hands, I made a mental note: in supply chain, there are no permanent relationships. Only *temporary perfection* until the next "strategic review."

9: The Reunion – Re-engagement

"Forgive, but don't forget the lead time."

Just when Sandeep thought he'd moved on, life — or rather, Q1 targets — had other plans.

It started with **Hariharan's wallet**. Not the metaphorical one, the *literal* one. It somehow ended up in the washroom during a vendor meeting. Inside were: three loyalty cards, an expired gym pass, and a sticky note labeled "Say yes to everything Sandeep asks."

Sandeep (holding the wallet): "So much for 'transparent partnerships.'"

The cracks had begun. Shipments were delayed. Emails were "lost." One consignment had packaging that looked like it had been through a toddler's birthday party.

That's when **Roshan** resurfaced — casually, like an ex bumping into you at a conference buffet.

Roshan (smiling): "Long time, Sandeep bhai. I heard your current supplier uses Comic Sans in invoices?"

Sandeep (sighing): "They also shipped us conditioner instead of chemical stabilizer last week."

And so, the *negotiated nostalgia* began.

Me (watching this unfold quietly): "Plot twist incoming."

Sandeep found himself in the world's most awkward Google Meet — with both **Roshan** and **Hariharan** on screen.

Roshan: "Look, I know we had issues... but our pallets were never 'moisturized.'"

Hariharan (defensive): "Innovation, Sandeep-ji. That's what that was."

Sandeep: "Guys... I need both of you. Roshan for the Q2 rush orders. Hariharan for the audits. Let's... share the wallet."

The silence was legendary. You could hear Roshan blinking in disbelief.

Thus began a *poly-vendor* relationship. Excel sheets were renamed "Blended Partnership Strategy." Slack channels were created titled "Neutral Zone."

Comic moments followed. Roshan and Hariharan tried to outdo each other in packaging designs. One included a custom thank-you poem. The other? Bubble wrap shaped like Sandeep's initials.

Sandeep (rubbing his temples): "I just wanted on-time delivery. Not fan art."

Eventually, everyone settled into the new normal — chaotic but functional. Roshan got his second chance, Hariharan learned humility, and Sandeep? Well, he became the first known buyer to pull off a successful vendor reunion *without HR involvement*.

Me (as I logged it in my silent ledger):

In supply chain, like in love — some relationships deserve a second life. With stricter SLAs.

The Laughing Ledger

Supplier: "Our latest product is a game-changer!"

Buyer: "Perfect, now change the price too!"

The Final Dispatch – Why Supplier-Buyer Relationships Matter

"Behind every successful company is a supplier who didn't mess up the delivery date."

After all the emails, Excel sheets, escalations, discount debates, and slightly-too-personal jokes on vendor calls, one thing becomes painfully — and comically — clear: the relationship between supplier and buyer is not just transactional. It's foundational.

Sure, on paper it looks like a simple supply chain flow. But in reality? It's a chaotic comedy where both parties juggle logistics, lead times, and emotions like overcaffeinated circus performers.

Roshan (Supplier): "We manufacture on-time delivery. But we also manufacture excuses. Both are on the product list."

Sandeep (Buyer): "We manage expectations. Mostly by lowering them."

Let's be honest — suppliers and buyers are like an old married couple running a convenience store. One handles the inventory, the other handles the customers, and both secretly blame each other for that missing carton of detergent.

But despite the jokes, when this relationship works, *everything works*:

Products reach the market on time.

Costs are optimized.

Inventory doesn't resemble a post-apocalyptic wasteland.

And most importantly — no one is yelled at on Monday morning Zoom calls.

When the supplier understands the buyer's business needs — not just the PO number — magic happens. When the buyer treats the supplier as a partner, not a punching bag, trust builds. And when both remember that *they are on the same side of the ERP system*, they align not just for targets, but for growth.

Me (observing with my cup of cold office tea):

"Sandeep and Roshan fought like in-laws, but shipped like legends."

The funny part? Most buyer-supplier conflicts aren't about capabilities. They're about communication. Misunderstood expectations. Misaligned priorities. And sometimes... a supplier calling at 6:01 PM on a Friday with "just a small urgent request."

So here's the serious message hiding in all the laughter: *Strong supplier-buyer relationships aren't built on contracts. They're built on conversations.*

Talk. Align. Deliver. Repeat.

Because when this duo dances in sync, the whole organization moves to the rhythm of success — with fewer delivery mishaps, more coffee breaks, and only the occasional meltdown over carton labelling.

HR & Employee

"HR is like Wi-Fi. You only notice them when something's not working."

It all started with an innocent Teams message.

Nikita (HR Manager): "Hey Manasi, quick question — can we hop on a 10-minute call?"

Manasi (Sales Executive): *[Internally screaming]* "What did I do? Am I getting fired? Did they find out about the printer incident?!"

What followed was a 47-minute video call about the *importance of work-life balance* and *updating your emergency contact number*. No one got fired. But Manasi did leave the call feeling like she needed a day off to recover from the stress of thinking she was about to be fired.

And that, dear reader, is the essence of HR.

They aren't just the folks behind the emails that start with "Dear All" and end with mandatory e-learning links. They're the office therapists (without a license), compliance officers, birthday cake coordinators, and part-time punching bags for every frustrated employee who's ever uttered the words, "Why do we even have HR?"

The relationship between HR and employees is a cocktail of confusion, contradictions, and compulsory feedback forms. When you first join, HR is your fairy godmother — sprinkling orientation decks, meal coupons, and ID cards like corporate confetti. A few months in, they transform into policy oracles, quoting leave clauses and dress code violations with unsettling precision.

And yet, somewhere between the awkward appraisal talks and team-building games that nobody wants to play, they're also your closest ally — especially when you're caught between two managers debating whether you need to work on a national holiday or just reply to emails from home "as per flexibility."

HR speaks a language of its own:

"We'll take it offline" = "I don't want to deal with this now."

"We hear you" = "We heard you... we're still ignoring you."

"Culture fit" = "You didn't laugh at the boss's joke, you monster."

In this chapter, we dive into the hilarious and heartfelt dynamics between HR and employees. From onboarding to offboarding, conflict resolution to cold policy emails, appraisals to exit interviews — it's a rollercoaster powered by Excel sheets, HRMS portals, and passive-aggressive CCs.

You'll meet HR Manager **Nikita**, who juggles between organizing Diwali décor and dealing with complaints about stolen tiffins. You'll also meet employees like **Manasi**, who believe HR's true role is to make sure your birthday gets exactly 17 claps in the breakout area.

So buckle up — or better yet, strap on your lanyard — as we take you through the real stories behind the smiles, the signatures, and the "as per company policies". Because in corporate life, HR isn't just a department — it's a survival strategy.

Let the passive-aggression begin.

The Laughing Ledger

HR: "We're like a family here!"

Employee: "Yeah, a dysfunctional one with too many meetings and not enough vacations!"

Sanket
AGARKAR

1.   The Welcome Wagon: Onboarding Day

Day one: when dreams meet policy documents.

There she was — **Manasi**, freshly ironed formalwear, anxiety packed into her laptop bag, eyes full of hope… and also a little confusion about whether she was supposed to bring her own pen.

Enter **Nikita**, HR Manager Extraordinaire, armed with a megawatt smile and a welcome kit heavy enough to require wheels.

Nikita: "Welcome to the family! This is your ID, your handbook, your meal coupons, your onboarding checklist, your IT access form, your form to acknowledge the checklist, and a fun little thing we call... the culture deck!"

Manasi (squinting at the culture deck): "Why does it feel like a PowerPoint with Stockholm Syndrome?"

Nikita: "Oh! You noticed the mascot — we call him 'Value Vinay'!"

As your silent observer, I stood at the corner of the room, sipping lukewarm onboarding-day chai, watching Manasi's face shift through all five stages of employment acceptance: excitement, confusion, regret, resignation, and finally... snack appreciation.

The onboarding ritual unfolded like a ceremony. Nikita projected enthusiasm with the energy of a motivational speaker at a multi-level marketing event.

Nikita: "At our company, we don't just *work*, we *thrive*! We *collaborate*! We *innovate*!"

Manasi: "We... haven't even gotten our Outlook passwords yet."

The room echoed with awkward chuckles from fellow new joinees, all equally overwhelmed by the swirl of paperwork and terms like "organogram," "HRMS," and "performance enablement framework."

Then came the icebreaker activity.

Nikita: "Everyone, pick an animal that reflects your work style!"

Manasi (whispers to me): "I was gonna say 'cat' because I don't like talking to people before 10 AM, but I said 'dolphin' because I panicked."

The rest of the day went by in a daze of department introductions, awkward elevator nods, and trying to remember who reports to whom on the org chart that looked like a plate of spaghetti.

But amidst all the confusion, one thing was clear: onboarding isn't just paperwork and passwords. It's the first impression of the circus you've joined — and **HR is the ringmaster** with a smile, a checklist, and a deck full of values.

And so, as the projector cooled down and Manasi tucked her swag kit under the desk, I sipped my third chai and thought:

"Welcome to corporate. The Wi-Fi will disconnect every two hours, but the HR enthusiasm? Never."

The Laughing Ledger

HR: "We're like a big family here."

Employee: "A family that never stops emailing."

2. The Pulse Check: Surveys No One Fills

When 'anonymous' surveys make you feel... very seen.

It was a Tuesday — the kind of day that neither inspires ambition nor excuses procrastination. I was just returning from the pantry with a soggy biscuit when **Manasi** slumped into her seat like a sitcom character in slow motion.

Manasi: "Guess what just landed in my inbox?" **Me:** "A meeting cancelation?" **Manasi:** "Worse. A Pulse Survey. From Nikita. With a subject line that says, 'Your Voice Matters!'"

Ah yes. The **corporate engagement survey** — that sacred ritual where employees pretend to care, and HR pretends it's anonymous.

Soon, **Nikita** popped her head over the workstation partitions like a prairie dog with a mission.

Nikita: "Guys, have you filled out the pulse survey? It's totally anonymous and super important. Like a heart monitor for company morale!"

Manasi gave me the side-eye.

Manasi (muttering): "If morale had a pulse, it flatlined during Q4."

Nikita stood there with the patience of a kindergarten teacher waiting for toddlers to form a circle.

Nikita: "It only takes 3 minutes! Just rate your experience from 1 to 5." **Manasi:** "Emotionally or professionally?" **Nikita:** "Haha... both! Be honest but constructive!"

And just like that, Manasi clicked open the survey.

Question 1: *Do you feel valued at work?*

Manasi: "Define 'feel'... and 'valued'... and 'work'."

Question 2: *Do you feel your voice is heard?*

Manasi: "Only when I sneeze during all-hands."

Question 3: *How likely are you to recommend this company to a friend?*

Manasi: "Depends. Do I like that friend or not?"

She hovered over the 'Submit' button like it was a trapdoor.

Me: "Just don't use words like 'toxic' or 'trapped in an emotional pyramid scheme.'" **Manasi:** "Right. I'll stick to 'room for growth' and 'needs clarity.'"

Two hours later, Nikita sent a *gentle nudge* email to everyone who hadn't responded.

Subject Line: "Gentle Reminder: Your Voice Still Matters 😊"

And beneath that was a spreadsheet titled **"Anonymous Survey Tracker.xlsx"**, shared... with names.

By the end of the day, Manasi and I sat at our desks, staring into the corporate void.

Manasi: "If my voice truly mattered, there'd be better coffee and fewer surveys." **Me:** "And meetings with biscuits that don't taste like regret."

As I watched Nikita cheerfully announce that 84% of employees feel "somewhat engaged," I realized:

Engagement surveys aren't about answers. They're about asking the questions HR already knows you won't answer honestly.

And still, every quarter, they try.

3. Policies & Procedures: The Gospel According to HR

Thou shalt not wear Crocs to Zoom calls... or live in peace.

It was one of those strange hybrid days — half work-from-home, half pretend-we're-in-the-office. Manasi had just logged into the morning huddle when her video popped up — framed perfectly, coffee in hand, productivity in spirit, **and bright yellow Crocs in full camera view.**

Nikita (HR, eyes narrowing): "Manasi… are those… Crocs?"
Manasi (cheerfully): "Yes! Sunshine yellow. Mood lifters. Limited edition." **Nikita:** "We do encourage professionalism on camera."

Manasi: "My head is professional. My feet are in Goa."

I watched from my muted square, quietly sipping tea. This was going to be fun.

Nikita didn't say anything at the time. But 43 minutes later, an all-employee email landed in our inboxes:

Subject: "Reminder: Remote Meeting Etiquette Guidelines 📌"

Attachment: *HR Policy_Rev7_FINAL_FINAL_UseThisOne.pdf*

This document was longer than most people's notice periods. It had clauses about digital backgrounds, "inappropriate slippers," and one oddly specific line:

"Employees must refrain from wearing Crocs, flip-flops, or inflatable pool accessories during official calls."

Manasi (in our private chat): "So… someone snitched. Or someone's allergic to comfort."

Later that day, Nikita casually dropped by Manasi's desk.

Nikita: "I hope the policy clarification email was helpful."

Manasi: "Very! I now know that my socks need to align with brand values."

Nikita smiled the way HR professionals do when they want to say "I'm watching you" but corporate laws won't let them.

Then came the *Policy Refresher Training* — 94 slides of joy, with interactive questions like:

Q: What should you wear during client meetings?

a) Suit

b) Blazer

c) Crocs

d) Regret

Meanwhile, Manasi started a secret Teams group called **"Policy Survivors Anonymous"**, where memes were shared like rations in a digital war.

Me (posting a meme): "HR policy says 'business casual'. My brain reads 'pajamas with intent.'"

By the end of the week, Nikita rolled out a *"Culture Alignment Quiz."* First question?

"If your footwear offends the client, what do you do?"

Manasi selected:

"Apologize and blame Wi-Fi."

HR policies may be written in corporate gospel, but they're lived through loopholes, interpretations, and well-timed memes.

And as your observer, I can confirm:

The war on Crocs continues.

4. **The Great Escape: Leave Management**

Applying for leave: A bureaucratic reality show where only one survives.

It was Wednesday. The sun had declared war on humanity, and Manasi had reached her boiling point — both professionally and thermally.

She popped into the HR bay like a polite storm cloud.

Manasi: "Hey Nikita, I was thinking of taking Friday off. Just need a break, recharge... maybe hydrate." **Nikita (without looking up):** "Why? It's just 35°C. Not 45°C." **Manasi:** "Yes, but emotionally, it feels like 52°C inside me."

I watched this unfold while sipping my fourth tea of the day — purely observational, of course.

Nikita (suspiciously): "You've already taken two leaves this quarter. We can't have a pattern forming." **Manasi:** "It's not a pattern; it's burnout prevention strategy."

That triggered the sacred HR protocol: *Form No. 12B — The Request for Planned Absence.*

It required:

A justification letter,

A backup plan,

Team alignment proof,

And a moral character certificate (okay, maybe not officially… but emotionally, yes).

Manasi (filling the form): "If I wanted to go to the Maldives, it would've been easier to apply for a visa."

Nikita reviewed the form with the seriousness of a loan officer at a risk committee.

Nikita: "This says 'mental detox' under reason." **Manasi:** "Yes. I'd like to remove the thoughts of MS Excel from my soul."

After 40 minutes, 3 policy documents, and a team group chat with replies like "If Manasi's out, who'll make the pitch deck?" (spoiler: not the person who sent that message), Nikita finally said:

Nikita: "Fine. One day. But only if you don't set an 'Out of Office' message that says 'Gone to find inner peace.'" **Manasi:** "Deal. I'll just say 'On personal pilgrimage to escape bandwidth.'"

By Friday, she was gone — and by 10:30 AM, so were five emails marked *URGENT - for Manasi.*

Me (quietly to myself): "She's free. For now."

Leave management is less about HR and more about negotiation, endurance, and dramatic storytelling.

You don't just *ask* for leave.

You *audition* for it.

And as your loyal observer — I can confirm:

If freedom has a price, it's payable in triplicate forms.

5. Conflict Resolution: The Therapy We Can't Afford

When office tempers flare, HR becomes the referee of a boxing match where both fighters wear business casual.

It started innocently enough. A campaign idea. A deck. A missing name in the "credits" section.

Manasi (storming into HR): "Nikita, I need a conflict resolution. Urgently. Emotionally. Legally, if possible." **Nikita (glancing up from her snack drawer):** "Okay… what happened this time?"

Manasi: "Pranav from marketing stole my idea. My idea! The 'Chai With Clients' concept was mine. He pitched it like it came to him in a dream. Yeah, my dream!"

As the designated silent observer, I adjusted my chair just slightly for a better view. Drama was about to steep like over-brewed green tea.

Nikita summoned Pranav. He arrived as if nothing had happened.

Pranav (grinning): "Hey Nikita. Hey Manasi. Did you see the client loved the Chai With Clients idea? Total hit, na?" **Manasi (deadpan):** "Glad my creativity is hydrating your ego."

Nikita sighed the sigh of every HR professional who didn't sign up for this but somehow became the office therapist.

Nikita: "Okay. Let's use the HR Mediation Framework." **Manasi:** "Does that involve a lie detector test?" **Nikita:** "No, it involves *talking like adults*, sharing perspectives, and resisting the urge to throw staplers."

They moved to the sacred HR conflict resolution room — a conference room with exactly one dead plant, one tissue box, and the mood lighting of a hostage negotiation scene.

Nikita: "Manasi, share how this situation made you *feel*." **Manasi:** "Like I was invisible in high resolution." **Nikita:** "And Pranav, any response?" **Pranav:** "I thought we were all brainstorming together. But okay, next time I'll put a trademark on her ideas."

An hour, one awkward silence, and three "let's align our energies" later...

Nikita: "So we agree to co-own the campaign and move forward?"
Manasi (gritting teeth): "Sure. As long as co-owning means I get top billing and he gets fonts duty."

HR conflict resolution is less therapy and more low-budget reality show.

There are no winners. Just people leaving the room slightly more bitter and slightly more polite.

And me? I'm just observing. With popcorn. And a notepad full of material.

6. Appraisals & Ambiguity

It's that magical season when employees dream big, write dramatic self-appraisals, and HR turns them into plot twists.

It began with an all-employee email titled **"Performance Review Cycle Begins – Let's Grow Together!"**

Manasi (muttering to herself): "Let's grow together? Last year I grew only horizontally from stress-snacking."

Two hours later, she was at her desk, crafting what could only be described as the *Oscar-winning script* of self-appraisals. Pages filled with KPIs, achievements, and cleverly disguised humblebrags.

Manasi (typing): "Demonstrated cross-functional collaboration by single-handedly saving the Q4 client meeting from collapse while handling three crisis calls and a torn shoe."

She submitted the self-appraisal with hope. Confidence. Delusion.

One week later...

Nikita (calling Manasi into HR's den): "So, I've reviewed your appraisal." **Manasi (bright-eyed):** "Yes, isn't it glorious? The part about 'dynamic initiative-taking in the face of shifting priorities'— that was a real moment, right?" **Nikita (softly):** "We had to normalize the ratings."

You could hear the crack in Manasi's soul from across the floor.

Manasi: "Normalize? What am I, a statistical anomaly?" **Nikita:** "Your 4.5 is now a 3.2. It's part of the bell curve." **Manasi:** "So is my enthusiasm. Dead centre of disappointment."

I watched as Manasi stared into the void—the HR wall with inspirational quotes printed in Comic Sans. Irony never looked so bold.

Nikita (gently): "It's not a reflection of your performance. It's a system process."

Manasi: "So the system thinks I'm average?"

Nikita: "No no. The system thinks *everyone* is average. That's equality."

And just like that, the self-worth she'd inflated during her "Achievements" section began to deflate like a party balloon in HR's storage closet.

Manasi: "Next year, I'm writing my self-appraisal in haiku. At least I'll get creative points."

Appraisal season is like corporate astrology—no matter what stars you align, you're still a Gemini with a 3.2.

The cycle ends with a polite handshake, vague promises of "next year will be better," and employees updating their LinkedIn in incognito mode.

7. The Whispers: Internal Complaints

Because no workplace drama is complete without a little anonymous backstabbing and carefully worded feedback.

It started with a *ding* on Manasi's laptop.

Subject: **"We Need to Talk – HR"**

She looked at me across the cubicle wall like a character in a true-crime documentary.

Manasi (whispering): "I didn't murder anyone. Yet."

She cautiously walked into **Nikita's** office—the HR sanctum that always smelled faintly of lavender and impending doom.

Nikita (smiling with concern): "Hi Manasi, just a quick catch-up."

Manasi (narrowing her eyes): "If this is about my secret stash of samosas in drawer 3, I've already eaten the evidence."

Nikita: "No no. We received... some feedback." **Manasi:** "Anonymous?" **Nikita:** "Yes. Completely. Though it does mention your desk location, the framed photo of your cat Ginger, and that your Spotify playlist is 87% Taylor Swift."

Manasi: "Wow. Anonymous feedback written by Sherlock Holmes."

Nikita slid a printout across the table like it was a classified file.

The Laughing Ledger

HR: "We care about employee well-being."

Employee: "Is that why you scheduled a 5 PM meeting?"

Anonymous Complaint #472:

"Manasi's laughter disrupts serious work. Also, her daily 3:05 pm humming of 'Love Story' causes mild irritation to colleagues."

Manasi (gasps): "That's my *focus hum*! It helps me think!"

Nikita: "And yet, it appears others prefer silence... or perhaps a more neutral tune." **Manasi:** "What do they want me to hum— Gregorian chants?!"

Meanwhile, I sat quietly outside HR, sipping tea and watching as the door shut with that soft, padded HR thud. The kind that means, "We're not mad, we're just disappointed."

The "anonymous" nature of such complaints is always up for debate. It's like an open secret—everyone knows who wrote it, no one admits it, and HR plays along like an underpaid UN peacekeeper.

Nikita (softly): "We just request you be a bit more mindful of... acoustics." **Manasi:** "Next time I'll just whisper Taylor Swift lyrics directly into their souls."

Internal complaints are like HR's version of fan mail—except no one's a fan, and everyone wants an autograph on a PIP.

And in this drama?

I remain the audience. Watching the stage.

Popcorn in hand. Noise-cancelling headphones on.

8. Training or Tragedy

Mandatory training: where enthusiasm goes to die and PDFs come to live forever.

It was a Tuesday. Which is to say, the day HR decided we all needed "mandatory learning."

The calendar invite read:

"Ethical Conduct Training – Mandatory. Attendance will be recorded. So will your silence."

Manasi leaned over the partition, clutching her coffee like it was a sedative.

Manasi: "Mandatory training again. What is it this time— 'how not to steal staplers?"

We filed into the meeting room (and by that I mean logged into Zoom with our cameras firmly off). **Nikita**, of course, was chipper—as all HR folks are, moments before delivering soul-crushing content.

Nikita: "Hi everyone! Welcome to today's exciting session on *Ethical Conduct in the Workplace!*" **Manasi (in chat, privately to me):** "Define exciting. I just watched paint dry and it blinked first."

Slide 1: *"Integrity is doing the right thing even when no one is watching."*

Slide 2: *"Don't claim sick leave while on a beach in Goa."*

Nikita: "Any real-life examples of ethical dilemmas?" **Manasi:** "Asking for a friend—if you *accidentally* click 'Mark as Complete' on a training before actually attending... is that unethical or just efficient?"

There was a long silence. Nikita blinked twice. HR blink-code for *noted for appraisal season*.

As the session dragged on, people started responding with emojis, just to prove they were alive. One brave soul even unmuted to ask:

Employee: "Will there be a quiz?" **Nikita:** "Yes, but it's just to reinforce learning." **Manasi:** "Or to identify future criminals, got it."

Later, as we all pretended to be captivated by Slide 12 (*"Respecting Confidentiality – Why You Shouldn't BCC Your Crush"*), I watched Manasi scribble in her notebook.

Me: "Notes?" **Manasi:** "No, it's a resignation letter disguised as doodles."

When the session ended (three hours later, but time had no meaning), Nikita cheerfully said:

Nikita: "Thanks for participating! Please fill the feedback form—constructive feedback only." **Manasi (muttering):** "I'll construct a whole wall to block future invites."

Corporate trainings are like microwaved popcorn: promising, slow, and mostly full of air. But hey, we all checked the box. Ethically, of course.

And me?

Still watching.

Still nodding.

Still not clicking "Mark as Complete" ... too early.

The
Laughing
Ledger

"HR emails: 'Your feedback is valuable to us'—but nothing will change!"

9. The Last Lap: Exit Interviews

"Because nothing says closure like a polite post-mortem of your corporate soul."

It was Manasi's last week.

The pantry had already seen two secret farewell samosas in her honour. Her laptop was slowly shedding files, and her locker had finally been emptied of stress balls and passive-aggressive post-its. And then came the final rite of passage: the **Exit Interview**.

Location: Conference Room

Attendees: Manasi and Nikita

Observer: Me, strategically seated near the coffee machine, holding a mug and a smirk.

Nikita: "Thanks for joining, Manasi. This will be a confidential, non-judgmental space for feedback." **Manasi:** "Of course. I've always dreamed of being brutally honest in a polite tone."

Nikita pulled out a printed form thicker than most onboarding kits.

Nikita: "So, what led you to explore opportunities outside?" **Manasi:** "Curiosity. Sanity. And the realization that coffee can't solve everything."

Nikita (smiling): "What could we have done better as an organization?" **Manasi:** "Shorter meetings. Longer lunch breaks. And maybe fewer 'all-hands' that achieve nothing except all-yawns."

Nikita noted something on her form. Possibly *future HR threat.*

Nikita: "How would you describe your experience here?"

Manasi: "Like a relationship that started with flowers and ended in group chats."

Nikita: "Any thoughts on management?" **Manasi:** "Rajiv is great! He taught me patience. Mostly by sending emails at 11:59 PM."

As the questions rolled on, Manasi leaned back, half-nostalgic, half-traumatized.

Manasi: "You know, I did learn a lot here." **Nikita:** "That's lovely to hear." **Manasi:** "Like how to mute myself while venting. And how to smile through 'noted.'"

Nikita: "Would you consider rejoining us in the future?" **Manasi:** "Sure. Right after HR adds 'power naps' to the benefits package."

After a few final checkboxes and a side conversation about her notice period's leftover leaves (which HR will definitely *not* encash without an email chase), it was over.

Exit interviews are like break-up conversations with someone who still wants to be friends.

HR listens. The employee politely burns bridges using scented words.

And somewhere between the feedback and the farewell cake, both parties quietly agree:

"We'll do better. Somewhere else."

And me? Still sipping coffee. Still observing. Still not filling my own exit form... yet.

HR & Employee — A Marriage of Complications

If corporate life were a sitcom, HR would be the responsible spouse trying to keep the household (read: workplace) from becoming a reality show. And employees? We're the unpredictable partner constantly testing boundaries, stealing the blanket of company policy, and secretly Googling "How to fake an emergency to skip a team-building activity."

It's a love-hate relationship built on Excel sheets, emotional escalations, and e-learning modules that no one completes.

HR says "we care about your growth," while sending you a 96-slide training titled *'How Not to Be Toxic in Teams.'*

Employees say "we appreciate HR," while simultaneously muting all HR announcements and rolling eyes at every new policy titled *"Work-Life Harmony Guidelines 5.0."*

It's give and take.

HR gives: policies, policies, and policies.

Employees take: all the sick leaves during long weekends.

But deep down, it works. Just like any marriage that runs on passive-aggressive Post-Its and anniversary emails with awkward cake-cutting ceremonies.

Comic Flashback Moments:

HR says, "Please be honest in your feedback."

You say, "I will."

HR gasps when you actually are.

HR: "We've scheduled an employee engagement session this Saturday!"

Employees: "Ah, the romance is dead."

Nikita from HR posts *"Wellness is wealth"* on Teams.

Manasi replies with a meme of someone napping in a Zoom call.

But here's the beautiful irony:

HR tries to keep the *culture* alive, while employees try to survive it.

HR plants the seeds of work-life balance, and we water it with caffeine and sarcasm.

Yet somehow, this odd couple keeps the engine running.

HR is the duct tape holding chaotic creativity, delayed appraisals, and 3-month notice periods together.

They're not just policy police—they're therapists, teachers, event planners, complaint listeners, and when required... the bouncers of toxic energy.

Employees, on the other hand, bring the chaos, colour, and corporate drama that makes HR relevant in the first place.

So yes, the HR-employee bond is messy, hilarious, and occasionally involves eye-roll marathons.

But it's also what gives the workplace *balance*—between compliance and comfort, process and people.

After all, what's a marriage without a little drama?

And what's a company without HR? A WhatsApp group with payroll issues.

End scene. Cue HR's email:

Subject: Mandatory Happiness Survey – Please Fill Before 6 PM.

Corporate in India

*"We don't work under pressure. We thrive in it,
bathe in it, and call it 'flexibility.'"*

The Pressure-Cooker Paradise

It was a Tuesday morning. Or maybe Thursday. Honestly, in Indian corporate life, the days blur into each other like Excel sheets without borders. Sandeep was on his third cup of chai, his fourth Zoom call, and his fifth draft of the same presentation.

"Why are we changing the title again?" he asked.

Rajiv, his boss, responded with the calm intensity of a man who meditates while reading performance reviews.

"It just doesn't feel impactful. Let's call it 'Vision 360: Reinventing the Synergy of Synergies.'"

Sandeep blinked. "So... the same content, but with extra jargon?"

"Exactly! See, you're learning flexibility!"

And that, dear reader, is the unofficial motto of Indian corporate life: **Flexibility above all.**

In the corporate world, there's a unique phenomenon that's as common as chai during meetings—**pressure**. But in India, we don't just work under pressure. No, no. We **thrive** in it. We **bask** in it. In fact, we've raised the art of working under pressure to an **Olympic level**. Here, it's less about surviving the stress and more about rebranding it as "handling multiple priorities with ease."

An urgent report? A last-minute client call? A system crash five minutes before the quarterly review? Mere speed bumps. The Indian employee's response is an enthusiastic, "No problem sir, I'll manage."

Because here, pressure is not a burden. It's a **badge of honour**. The more you can smile through delayed deadlines, unreasonable expectations, and budget cuts masked as "growth optimization," the more you're seen as a corporate warrior.

Flexibility, in the Indian workplace, means being available for calls during dinner, changing entire presentations overnight, and replying to emails that start with "Just a small request..." but require three hours of your life. And all of this while attending your cousin's wedding on Zoom, fixing your Wi-Fi, and answering your boss on WhatsApp.

And yet, somehow—miraculously—it works.

Maybe it's the adaptability. Maybe it's the sheer force of jugaad. Or maybe it's the daily dose of caffeine, carbs, and chaos.

Whatever the secret sauce is, the Indian corporate ecosystem thrives in the sweet spot between absurdity and achievement.

So, fasten your seatbelts, grab your chai, and let's dive into this wild, wonderful, workaholic world through nine sub-chapters that reveal how we survive—not in spite of the pressure, but because of it.

1:   The Art of Juggling Deadlines

"Perfect. By tomorrow. But also now."

Deadlines in Indian corporate life are not rigid lines in the sand—they're more like shifting mirages. What begins as "end of the week" turns into "EOD," and then quietly slides into "Can we get it in the next 30 minutes?" It's a beautiful, chaotic circus act of juggling multiple tasks while blindfolded... on a unicycle... during an earthquake.

Take Dhaval, our star performer, the unofficial corporate magician. No matter the crisis, he delivers. He could be presenting on one laptop, designing on another, and troubleshooting a printer with his feet—and somehow, he'd still meet his deadlines.

One fine Monday, Rajiv—the ever-demanding, spreadsheet-loving boss—stormed into the war room (which was really just a conference room with bad lighting).

Rajiv: "Dhaval, the client just pushed the review up to tomorrow morning. We'll need the final version tonight."

Dhaval (without looking up): "I've already sent it."

Rajiv paused, confused.

Rajiv: "But I haven't even briefed you yet."

Dhaval: "I had a feeling this would happen. I used your favorite buzzwords: synergy, agility, and digital-first. You're welcome."

From the other end of the room, I sipped my chai and watched Rajiv struggle between admiration and mild professional jealousy. His eyebrow twitched—the only visible sign of emotion.

Rajiv: "Let's aim to make it perfect."

Dhaval: "It already is. But I can run it through ChatGPT again if you'd like some extra adjectives."

Meanwhile, Sandeep, the overly enthusiastic sidekick, tried to jump in.

Sandeep: "Sir, if Dhaval's too tied up, I can also take a crack at it!"

Rajiv (without turning): "Let's not reinvent the wheel, Sandeep."

Sandeep (muttering): "But I *am* the wheel."

The truth is, in Indian offices, the concept of "deadline" comes with three unspoken clauses:

It's flexible. But not really.

It's urgent. But not final.

It's communicated politely, but means "do it yesterday."

Under the glow of flickering tube lights and buzzing WhatsApp groups, people like Dhaval keep the show running. While everyone else is either panicking, pretending to panic, or panic-Googling templates, Dhaval simply delivers.

And Rajiv? He goes back to his corner office, comforted by the illusion of control. After all, deadlines are only scary if you don't have a Dhaval on your team.

And me? I just watch... with popcorn.

2: PowerPoint Presentations and Spiritual Rebirth

"Thou shalt beautify thy deck... or face the wrath of Rajiv."

In Indian corporate life, PowerPoint presentations are more than visual aids—they're a sacred ritual, an emotional rollercoaster, and a test of inner strength. Crafting a deck isn't just work; it's a spiritual journey through purpose, pain, and pixel alignment.

It all began one unusually peaceful Tuesday morning. The AC was humming, the chai was hot, and for a brief moment, everything felt right. Until Rajiv entered.

Rajiv (with that "I-have-a-deck-idea" gleam in his eye): "Team, we need to create a presentation for the CEO's strategy meeting. Something powerful. Something moving. I want the CEO to be *speechless*."

Sandeep, ever enthusiastic and occasionally clueless, jumped in.

Sandeep: "Got it, sir. I'll throw in a couple of graphs, a picture of a puppy, and a motivational quote from Steve Jobs."

Rajiv (nodding gravely): "Perfect. But make it soulful. Something that tells a story. Something that says, 'We are more than just KPIs.'"

Dhaval, who had been quietly sipping his protein shake, slowly looked up.

Dhaval: "Are we presenting strategy or manifesting our inner chakras?"

Rajiv: "Both. And don't forget transitions. The CEO likes 'Zoom In' for impact."

That marked the beginning of what I now refer to as "Deck-pocalypse."

What followed was a 14-hour, soul-draining marathon where slide titles were changed thrice, fonts were debated like government policy, and three separate versions of the same pie chart were created—each with a different shade of blue.

By 9 PM, Dhaval was meditating between slides 14 and 15, questioning the meaning of life.

Sandeep, on the other hand, had created a 52-slide epic titled *"The Synergy of Synergy"* which Rajiv rejected after slide 2 for being "too circular."

Rajiv (frustrated): "We're not doing a TED Talk, Sandeep! Just show growth, opportunity, and... emotion."

Sandeep: "Should I add background music?"

Dhaval (deadpan): "Only if it's a funeral march."

Eventually, Dhaval stepped in, cleaned up the mess, and created a crisp 12-slide deck that told a story, showcased data, and even had a subtle nod to emotional intelligence.

Rajiv (finally smiling): "Now *this* is what I'm talking about."

And me? I watched it all unfold with the kind of quiet reverence usually reserved for wildlife documentaries. Because here in the Indian corporate jungle, PowerPoint isn't just a tool—it's a path to enlightenment.

Slide by slide, we are reborn.

The Laughing Ledger

"Corporate work: Where your LinkedIn profile looks much happier than your actual day-to-day life!"

Sanket
AGARKAR

3: The 'Late-Night' Productivity

"We don't burn out—we burn the midnight oil."

There's a peculiar charm to the Indian corporate office at night. The daytime chaos simmers down, the boss's voice echoes a little less, and there's a strange peace broken only by the soft *ting* of incoming emails and the buzzing of the coffee machine on its third wind.

It was 9:47 PM on a Wednesday. Technically "end of the day." But in reality, it was just halftime.

Rajiv walked past our desks with a mug of green tea and the energy of a man who had just found a typo in someone else's report.

Rajiv: "Team, I know it's late, but I've just had a brilliant thought. Let's rethink the deck strategy. Something more... organic."

Dhaval, the star performer and unwilling night owl, blinked twice and looked at his watch.

Dhaval: "Sir, it's almost 10 PM."

Rajiv (inspiring mode): "Exactly! This is the golden hour. Brain is quiet, distractions are minimal, Wi-Fi is strong."

Meanwhile, Manasi from sales had just microwaved her fourth cup of chai.

Manasi: "I'm just getting into the zone."

Nikita from HR peeked in from a Teams call titled "Employee Wellbeing."

Nikita: "Guys, don't forget work-life balance."

Manasi (deadpan): "This *is* my work-life zone now."

I watched as the lights flickered slightly—either the office building was haunted by overworked souls, or the inverter was also done for the day.

Across the floor, tired eyes stared at screens, tapping away furiously. Someone whispered, "Dinner's here." A cheer erupted—not for food, but because it meant someone remembered to *order*.

Rajiv stood tall, dramatically observing the team.

Rajiv: "You know, Steve Jobs once said, 'The only way to do great work is to love what you do.'"

Dhaval: "Did Jobs also mention when we can go home?"

Rajiv chuckled, mistaking sarcasm for spirit.

By midnight, things got philosophical.

Manasi: "If I work from 9 AM to 12 AM, does that mean I've covered two workdays in one?"

Dhaval: "Only if you clock it twice in the HRMS."

Somewhere between the fourth draft of the deck and the third delivery of biryani, productivity did emerge—sleep-deprived, caffeine-fueled, and slightly delusional.

Because in Indian corporates, the real productivity doesn't start at 9 AM. It hits after sunset, when the city sleeps and your inbox lights up like Diwali.

Work-life balance? Nah. We believe in *work-life blend*, with a side of Maggi and moral support.

The Laughing Ledger

"Corporate holidays: Days when you just work from home in pajamas instead of the office."

Sanket
AGARKAR

4: The 'Client-Focused' Emergency

"The client is always right—even when they're wrong, confused, or calling at 11:57 PM."

It was a typical Tuesday evening—or as we fondly call it, *pre-emergency calm*. The office was winding down. Spoons clinked in tea cups. Manasi from sales was humming a romantic song from the '90s, Dhaval was speed-scrolling LinkedIn pretending to "research industry trends," and I, the quiet observer, was mentally drafting my resignation letter—just for fun.

Then the air shifted. A storm was coming. And it had a name: **Rajiv.**

Rajiv: "Everyone, urgent client request. I need all hands on deck."

Dhaval: "Didn't the client presentation get over this morning?"

Rajiv: "Yes. But they just remembered they needed 'something extra.'"

Manasi: "Define 'extra'?"

Enter Ahmed, the ever-dramatic Sales Manager, phone in hand, face like he'd seen a ghost holding a deadline.

Ahmed: "The client wants a fresh proposal deck with revised pricing, competitor benchmarking, updated case studies, and—get this—a one-minute explainer video."

Dhaval blinked. "By when?"

Ahmed: "By 9 AM tomorrow."

Dhaval: "What year?"

Just then, Sales Head **Vikram** burst in with the energy of a Bollywood villain entering a climax scene.

Viram: "Team, this is critical. The client is evaluating two vendors. If we miss this, it goes to the other guy."

Rajiv (nodding wisely): "This is a defining moment. Let's show them our agility."

Dhaval (muttering): "More like, let's define insomnia."

Manasi: "I'll call the design guy."

Ahmed: "He's on leave."

Manasi: "Then I'll design it. How hard can Canva be?"

The air turned into caffeine. Laptops opened. WhatsApp pings exploded. Everyone moved with the precision of soldiers—but with more passive-aggressive sighing.

At 1:42 AM, we had a deck. At 2:13, the video was "decent enough." At 3:05, Manasi fell asleep on her keyboard and accidentally typed "aaaaaa" into the client's name field.

Rajiv: "This is what teamwork looks like. I'm proud of you all."

Dhaval: "Does pride come with comp-off?"

The deck was sent. The email was marked "High Importance." The client replied at 9:47 AM.

Client: "Thanks! Let's connect next week. No hurry."

We sat in silence. Eyes bloodshot. Coffee cups empty. Spirit... debatable.

But in Indian corporates, this is what we call *flexibility*: responding to flexible urgency with even more flexible sanity.

5:   The Myth of 'Work-Life Balance'

"In Indian corporates, 'me-time' is just the time between two Teams calls."

The sun was high, and so was everyone's blood pressure. Lunch hour had technically started, but in our office, "lunch hour" was more of a mythical concept—like a unicorn with a coffee addiction. I had just opened my tiffin when I heard the unmistakable sound of Boss Rajiv's "announcement tone."

Rajiv (striding into the floor like a TED Talk was due): "Team, remember — balance is key! You must take breaks. Enjoy life!"

Dhaval (half-chewing a dry roti): "Sir, I just stepped away for five minutes and returned to four emails, two missed calls, and a Slack ping asking where I was."

Rajiv (smiling): "That's good! Shows you're important."

Dhaval: "I'd like to be unimportant for just twenty uninterrupted bites."

Enter Sandeep, dishevelled, holding a half-filled plate and a full inbox.

Sandeep: "Sir, I tried to eat, but the client asked for a 'quick update call.' Now I'm explaining logistics while chewing paratha."

Rajiv (nodding): "Flexibility! That's what sets us apart. We're adaptable warriors."

Sandeep (whispering): "Warriors get armor. We get weak Wi-Fi and cold lunch."

Meanwhile, HR sent out a cheerful email with the subject line: *"Reclaim Your Lunch Breaks!"* Inside it read, *"Take your break between 1:00 and 2:00 PM—unless of course, you're in a client call, escalation meeting, or chasing numbers."*

Dhaval: "So basically, we can reclaim our lunch break... in theory."

The office microwave became a symbol of lost dreams. Every time someone approached it, their phone buzzed. Every. Single. Time.

Manasi (on call with a fork in hand): "Yes, sir, I'll send the proposal... No, not you sir, I was talking to my dal."

Rajiv passed by and declared, "Look at this dedication! Eating while working. That's the spirit of multitasking!"

Dhaval (under breath): "One more compliment like that and I'll start eating my appraisals."

By evening, the word "balance" had been used eight times in motivational emails, zero times in practice.

In Indian corporates, "work-life balance" is not a right. It's a Rubik's cube—brightly colored, impossible to solve, and always one turn away from perfect. But somehow, we keep twisting, turning, and surviving on chai and hope.

6: Pressure Equals Innovation

"Innovation is just panic in disguise—with PowerPoint."

There's a myth that creativity needs calm, serenity, and long walks in the garden. In India? Creativity needs a deadline, a panic attack, and a boss breathing down your neck like a motivational foghorn.

It was 5:42 PM on a Friday—also known as the worst possible time to start anything new. Yet, that's precisely when the Sales Head, Vikram, strolled onto the floor with a glint in his eye and a PowerPoint deck in hand.

Vikram (dramatically): "Team! We need to launch a campaign by Monday. Bold, disruptive, exciting."

Manasi (blinking): "Monday? As in... the next Monday?"

Vikram: "Yes. Innovation thrives under urgency! Remember Jugaad? It's in our DNA."

I watched as Manasi's pupils dilated from shock to sarcasm.

Manasi: "Do we have a brief? A budget? A direction?"

Vikram (beaming): "We have passion. And a Google Drive folder titled '2020 Campaign Ideas – Revise Maybe.'"

Thus, began what can only be described as a caffeine-fueled sprint through chaos. Manasi sat with a notepad, sketching out campaign ideas while sipping on her fourth chai. Vikram, meanwhile, circled the team like a motivational hawk.

Vikram: "Think outside the box!"

Manasi: "Sir, the box left the building. We're now deep inside a paper bag filled with budget cuts."

The whiteboard quickly filled with arrows, diagrams, and quotes like "Urgency is the mother of invention." Someone accidentally wrote a pricing chart in Manasi's planner. Sandeep dropped in briefly, offered a confused thumbs-up, and vanished.

By Saturday morning (because weekends are illusions), the team had a prototype, a presentation, and three memes ready to pitch.

Vikram (proudly): "You see? Pressure creates diamonds."

Manasi (exhausted): "I think it also caused a mild stroke, but sure, sparkle away."

The campaign was pitched Monday morning. It wasn't perfect— but it was bold, disruptive, and held together with duct tape and last-minute inspiration.

In Indian corporates, the pressure cooker isn't just in the kitchen. It's in every project. But give a desi employee a ticking clock, a missing budget, and a vague brief—and they'll still pull off a miracle. Probably while finishing a plate of poha.

Because here, pressure isn't a problem. It's a platform.

7: The Unofficial Overtime Ritual

"It's not overtime if no one clocks it."

In Indian corporate life, there's a sacred tradition that unfolds post 6:30 PM—the time when most of the world heads home, and Indian employees... order another cutting chai. Welcome to the unofficial overtime ritual. Not mentioned in offer letters. Not tracked in attendance software. But deeply etched into our office carpets and under-eye circles.

It was one of those long Tuesdays disguised as a Friday. The lights were dim, laptops were glowing, and the office AC had decided to switch to *Arctic Tundra* mode.

Nikita (HR, doing a floor walk): "Hi everyone! Just a gentle reminder to maintain work-life balance."

Vikram (Sales Head, peering from his glass cabin): "Yes, balance it after this deck is done."

Manasi (Sales Executive, yawning): "Technically, this is life. It's just that the Wi-Fi is faster than my heartbeat."

I watched as Manasi adjusted her desk plant to use it as a makeshift pillow. Her screen had five tabs open—three with sales reports, one with Excel macros, and one YouTube tab on mute playing "Lo-Fi Beats to Cry To."

Nikita: "Manasi, you've been here since 9 AM. It's almost 9 PM now!"

Manasi: "Don't worry, Nikita. I took a break at 2:15. I blinked for a full five seconds."

Meanwhile, Sandeep strolled in with samosas and that odd confidence of someone who's accepted that dinner will always be had at his desk.

Sandeep: "It's not overtime. It's passion work."

Vikram (nodding approvingly): "That's the spirit. You see, Nikita? This is what builds empires."

Nikita (sighing): "Empires of burnout, maybe."

No one leaves first. That's the unspoken code. Leaving early—or on time—is viewed with the same suspicion as saying "I don't drink chai." You might be called "not serious enough," or worse, "9-to-5 mentality."

So we all sit there, sipping chai, pretending to work, or actually working because *some* client just sent "one small change" at 8:47 PM.

By 10 PM, the office finally empties. One by one, the warriors pack up, high on adrenaline, fried snacks, and artificial lighting.

In India, overtime isn't just tolerated—it's romanticized. It's not about efficiency; it's about endurance. And while HR hangs posters about balance, the office culture proudly whispers, "If you're not working late, are you even part of the team?"

8: The 'Constant Revisions' Tango

"Version 23_Final_ReallyFinal_ThisOneForReal.pptx"

Revisions in Indian corporate life are like Bollywood plot twists—dramatic, frequent, and completely unpredictable. It doesn't matter if you've burned the midnight oil, sacrificed your lunch breaks, and aged emotionally—your deck, report, or plan will be sliced, diced, and seasoned with 15 different types of feedback by the time it reaches Version 23.

It was a usual Tuesday morning—or at least it started that way—until Rajiv, our ever-demanding boss, summoned Sandeep with an email that had the subject line: "Feedback – Urgent."

Sandeep (entering Rajiv's cabin): "Rajiv sir, you asked for me?"

Rajiv (smiling like a surgeon about to announce bad news): "Yes, Sandeep. I went through your report. Very solid effort."

Sandeep (relieved): "Oh, thank you, sir!"

Rajiv: "So I made a few minor suggestions."

Sandeep: "How many, sir?"

Rajiv: "Only 15. You'll find them in the 3 separate emails. One for structure, one for tone, and one just for vibes."

I was sitting at my desk nearby, sipping chai and pretending to focus, but watching this unfold was better than Netflix.

Sandeep walked out like a man who had just been told his baby wasn't cute enough.

Sandeep (mumbling): "Continuous improvement? I need continuous medication."

By 3 PM, Sandeep had updated the report with all of Rajiv's suggestions.

Rajiv (after skimming the revision): "Hmm… looking good. But I was thinking, what if we completely change the approach?"

Sandeep: "Sir… we changed the approach five times."

Rajiv: "Yes, but this time, let's keep it more dynamic. More strategic. More… less."

Sandeep: "More less?"

Rajiv: "Exactly! That's the thinking I want."

And just like that, Sandeep opened the file titled *Final_V17*, sighed deeply, and saved a new copy: *Final_V18_NoSeriouslyThisTime.pptx*.

At one point, Rajiv suggested adding a "storytelling element," so Sandeep added a slide with a quote from Mahabharata and a meme of a raccoon holding coffee.

Rajiv: "Perfect! This is what I meant. Insight meets inspiration."

Sandeep: "Great. Glad Lord Krishna and the raccoon made the cut."

Revisions are like Indian street food—hot, spicy, and you never know what you're going to get. Flexibility here doesn't mean agreeing to changes; it means *embracing* them… even when they make no sense. Because in the end, it's not about the perfect file. It's about surviving till the version that no one has the energy to edit anymore.

9: The Power of Chai and Chat

"When in doubt, boil water, add tea leaves, and call it a team meeting."

In Indian corporates, one powerful ritual transcends departments, hierarchies, and deadlines—**the Chai Break**. It's our unofficial therapy session, mini-townhall, venting zone, and innovation hub—served hot in a paper cup.

It was 4:17 PM—known in our office as "Productivity Slump Hour." Emails were being ignored. Excel sheets were open but untouched. That's when HR Manager Nikita popped her head out of her glass cabin.

Nikita: "Let's take a five-minute tea break to clear our heads."

Sandeep (from his seat, not moving): "Isn't that your solution to every problem? Employee burnout? Tea. Deadline anxiety? Tea. Broken chair? Let's talk about it… over tea."

Nikita (grinning): "It's a *flexible* solution, Sandeep."

Before you could say "chai peene chalo," half the department had migrated like pigeons to the pantry. I, as usual, tagged along silently, mug in hand, soaking in the unfiltered wisdom of this gathering.

Dhaval (star performer, slurping his cutting chai): "I just submitted a 67-slide deck. I deserve this cup. And a raise."

Manasi (Sales executive, holding her cup like a trophy): "My client ghosted me all day. I emailed, called, sent memes. Nothing. But this chai? This won't disappoint me."

Sandeep: "We should rename the pantry to 'Corporate ICU'. We all come here to be revived."

Nikita (sipping thoughtfully): "You know what? No matter how stressful things get, one cup of tea, one round of harmless gossip, and we're back in the game."

Suddenly, Dhaval raised his cup like a toast.

Dhaval: "To chai—the real boss we all obey."

Manasi: "And to this five-minute break that always lasts twenty."

It was in this laughter-filled moment that I realized—**this** is where the *real* corporate bonding happens. Not in townhalls. Not in those 'fun engagement activities' that involve charades and awkward dancing. But here—in spontaneous jokes, biscuit sharing, and the shared sigh after sipping that first hot gulp.

In Indian corporate life, chai is more than a beverage—it's a **coping mechanism**, a **collaboration tool**, and sometimes the only reason people don't resign mid-week.

When the pressure rises, the dashboards crash, and the deadlines feel like doom—chai doesn't just refresh, it **resurrects**. And while work may never end, at least there's always time for one more cup.

The Fine Art of Thriving Under Pressure

Ah, the grand paradox of Corporate India—where we celebrate the chaos of deadlines, applaud the madness of last-minute tasks, and wear our stress like a badge of honor. Welcome to the world where pressure is not just a part of the job, it's the whole job description. It's the dance we've perfected over years, each pirouette more dramatic than the last.

You see, in India, we don't just *work* under pressure, we create art out of it. It's not about surviving; it's about *thriving* under the constant storm of urgent emails, ever-shifting goals, and the occasional project that magically appears in your inbox at 11 PM. It's all part of the *flexibility* culture.

Rajiv, the strict boss, often says:

"Let's aim for perfection, but also... flexibility."

Translation? "I want this report *yesterday*, and yes, I'll need you to add a puppy gif for good measure."

Sales Head Vikram loves the high-pressure environment. His mantra is:

"Push the limits!"

Translation? "Your weekend plans? They're now part of Q4. Have fun."

HR Nikita, the eternal optimist, tells us:

"Don't forget work-life balance!"

Translation? "Work through lunch. Here's a link to a breathing exercise that should have worked three hours ago."

And us? We've all become masters of squeezing an impossible amount of work into a time slot smaller than a chai break. The truth is, we are superheroes in disguise—fighting deadlines, answering emails, and holding everything together like it's the easiest thing in the world.

The Famous Corporate Punchlines (Reality Check):

"Just a quick update!" → "You'll need a week and a double shot of espresso."

"We need to discuss this further." → "You're staying late tonight. Let's chat after 9 PM."

"You're doing great!" → "But why is everything so late? Maybe try 'doing better' next time."

However, as much as we love the adrenaline rush of working under pressure, let's face it—burnout is real. The downside of thriving under pressure is that it doesn't leave room for balance, relaxation, or actually *living*.

Pressure may fuel creativity and innovation, but if we're always running on fumes, there's no room to breathe. Work-life balance isn't just a buzzword—it's the difference between being an employee and being a *zombie in a suit*. Keep the flexibility, but let's not forget to recharge. Because, in the end, even the best machines need downtime.

So, while pressure is the flavour of the day, let's add a little work-life balance to our corporate recipe. After all, burnout is not a badge of honour—it's the end of the show.

The Sacred Phrase: "As Discussed"

"If it was "discussed", it doesn't need to be documented. Until someone gets blamed."

THE ULTIMATE WEAPON

In the complex labyrinth of corporate life, there exists one phrase that defies the rules of time, bypasses the need for written communication, and floats above every email thread with an air of untouchable superiority: *"As discussed."* This phrase isn't just words—it's an unspoken weapon that allows you to skate across the treacherous waters of accountability, all while looking like you have everything under control. It's as if the phrase has magical properties: it's simultaneously vague and precise, casual yet commanding, and, above all, conveniently absent when you need documentation.

Let's face it: *"As discussed"* is the ultimate escape artist. It's the Houdini of corporate lingo, slipping out of the grasp of deadlines, documentation, and any real effort to clarify details. Whether you're in a meeting, a phone call, or a hallway chat, the words *"As discussed"* can cover everything, and yet, cover nothing at all. When you don't want to get bogged down by the hassle of writing things down, you just utter these words, and suddenly, everything's been handled— on paper, at least. But in reality, all you've done is create a grey zone where the line between what was agreed upon and what was imagined is as blurry as a foggy morning.

This phrase is a staple in every corporate survival kit. It's the tool of choice when you want to avoid the messy details of documentation or the hassle of fleshing out specifics. It gives you just enough leeway to act as though something was agreed upon—without having to prove it. It's the verbal equivalent of an invisible ink contract: you're both bound to it, but no one can really see what was written. And when something inevitably goes wrong, well, you can always circle back to the *"As discussed"* loophole to make it seem like the fault lies with someone else for not remembering.

It's used with such ease and frequency that it's practically sacred. Everyone from the CEO to the intern knows the power of this phrase, and more often than not, they wield it expertly. But beware—the phrase only works until the blame game starts. That's when the true cost of relying on *"As discussed"* comes to light, and the cracks in the façade start showing.

In this chapter, we'll dissect the art of *"As discussed"* and explore its nine distinct manifestations in the corporate world. Get ready to uncover how this phrase lives on the fine line between effective communication and corporate chaos.

1: The 'Don't Worry, It Wasn't That Important' Version

In the grand theatre of corporate life, one of the most powerful phrases ever uttered is *"As discussed."* This magical phrase holds the uncanny ability to transform a casual conversation into something that feels like an official decision, even when no one actually remembers what was discussed—or worse, if it wasn't discussed at all.

This is the version where *"As discussed"* is wielded like a cloak of invisibility to avoid the uncomfortable and tedious task of documenting anything. It's the perfect way to bypass email chains, paper trails, or the pesky act of putting things in writing. In these situations, it's not about the actual details; it's about giving the illusion that everything was crystal clear, even if everyone involved is now scrambling to figure out exactly what was agreed upon.

The
Laughing
Ledger

"As discussed" is the corporate version of "You should know this by now."

Rajiv (Boss): "Remember, as discussed, let's move the deadline to Friday." Sandeep (Employee): "Sure, Rajiv, but I never got an email on it." Rajiv (calmly): "It was all in the meeting, Sandeep. Just follow up on that."

Sandeep, trying to act calm but clearly confused, flips through his notes to find any mention of this alleged discussion. He finds nothing but a doodle of a cat with a moustache. "Okay, Rajiv," he says, nodding like he understood, but secretly wondering if he missed something in that meeting. The meeting that, apparently, involved a whole lot of *"discussing"* without anything ever being documented. Now, it's too late to go back and ask for an email—because doing so would imply that you weren't paying attention or, worse, that you weren't following the rules of corporate ambiguity.

Rajiv (in his element): "Look, Sandeep, it's not that important. You'll just get it done by Friday, right? No need for the paperwork. Trust me."

Sandeep (laughing nervously): "Sure, Rajiv. Friday sounds great. No worries at all. I'll just go... *wing it.*"

And just like that, the corporate machine rolls on. The phrase *"As discussed"* has done its job—it's dodged the need for any official communication and created just enough uncertainty to ensure that no one will question what was actually discussed. In fact, it's probably too late for anyone to go back and ask for a confirmation email. So, everyone shrugs, pretends to understand, and moves forward, all while secretly hoping that Friday won't be too much of a nightmare.

As we all know, this version of *"As discussed"* comes with a price: the price of never really knowing what was decided, but also never really needing to know. After all, in the corporate world, ambiguity is your best friend—especially when it's been *"discussed."*

The
Laughing
Ledger

"Corporate life in India:
Where your day starts
with traffic and ends with
'as discussed in the
meeting'."

Sanket
AGARKAR

2: The Unspoken Agreement

In the corporate world, sometimes *"As discussed"* serves a more mysterious, almost mystical purpose. It doesn't actually refer to anything formally discussed, agreed upon, or even vaguely mentioned in a meaningful way. No, no. Instead, it's a reference to a conversation that existed in the ether—a chat that may have lasted all of 10 seconds in passing, usually near the coffee machine, with a nod, a smile, and the faintest suggestion of a plan. Yet, somehow, *"As discussed"* transforms it into a binding agreement, or so everyone hopes.

The Laughing Ledger

No one remembers the discussion, but "as discussed" gives it legitimacy.

Imagine this scenario:

Rajiv (Boss): "As discussed, let's implement the new strategy starting next week." Sandeep (Employee, confused): "Did we really discuss this, Rajiv? I don't recall anything about it." Rajiv (with a confident smile): "Of course, we did. *As discussed*, remember? It's all settled."

Sandeep, in disbelief, frantically tries to recall the moment he agreed to this "new strategy." Did it happen in the 10 seconds before the coffee machine pran out of sugar? Or was it during that brief pause between the meeting about Q3 targets and Rajiv's impromptu monologue on the superiority of his favourite brand of pens? He's not sure, but now it's on his to-do list. And just like that, a new task has appeared, one that wasn't discussed at all—or maybe just in the same way you might mention what's for lunch.

Sandeep (faking confidence): "Right, yes, of course. New strategy. Got it. I'll start working on that right away."

Rajiv (nodding like a wise guru): "Great, Sandeep. I knew you'd take charge. It's all about following through on what we *discussed*."

Cue the awkward silence as Sandeep shuffles off, wondering how he can pull off implementing a strategy that didn't exist until five seconds ago.

In these situations, *"As discussed"* is corporate magic. There's no paper trail, no emails, and no solid plan—but suddenly, a new task has materialized out of thin air, and it's now part of your job description. The best part? There's no way to prove it wasn't actually "discussed," because, well, *someone* definitely remembers it, and that someone usually has the title of "Boss."

Sandeep, still scratching his head, wonders if *"As discussed"* is just an abstract concept—a corporate equivalent of "What happens in Vegas stays in Vegas," but with a lot more work to do. And so, the circle of confusion continues, all under the banner of *"As discussed."* The corporate world is truly magical—if only in its ability to turn a fleeting moment into an unspoken agreement.

As for me, the observer? Well, I just sit back, watch the magic unfold, and wait for the inevitable next "As discussed" moment.

3: The Escape Clause

Ah, the true power of *"As discussed"* is never clearer than when something goes horribly wrong—and no one wants to take the blame. Enter: *The Escape Clause.*

Picture this. It's Monday morning. Chaos brews like the office chai. Emails are flying, deadlines are dying, and somewhere in the corner sits Vikram, our seasoned boss, sipping his coffee like he's in a calm meditation retreat.

Suddenly, in walks Manasi—Sales Executive, caffeine-fuelled, anxiety-charged.

Manasi: "Vikram, wasn't this report supposed to go out last Friday?"

Vikram (smooth as silk): "Yes... *as discussed*, you were supposed to send it."

Manasi (frowning): "Wait, what? I thought you said you'd review it first?"

Vikram (channelling corporate Zen): "Of course, but *as discussed*, we agreed you'd take the lead. I believe I even mentioned it during the wrap-up meeting... in spirit."

And just like that, Manasi is trapped in the *Escape Clause*. She's mentally rewinding every conversation from the past two weeks, trying to locate this alleged discussion. But it's gone. It either never happened, or it happened in Rajiv's telepathic dream sequence.

I sit at my desk, watching this unfold like a Netflix dramedy.

Manasi sighs, opens her laptop, and mutters, "Fine, I'll send it now."

Vikram smiles like a man who's just successfully dodged responsibility with a single phrase.

Moral of the story? In the corporate blame game, documentation is optional. *"As discussed"* is eternal.

The Laughing Ledger

"As discussed"—the corporate equivalent of "You should've known better."

Sanket
AGARKAR

4: The Phantom Email

In every Indian corporate office, there exists a mystical phenomenon—**The Phantom Email**. It's the kind of email that exists only in verbal realms and manager memory. No one's actually seen it, no one's received it, and yet, everyone is expected to act on it. It's like Bigfoot, but in Outlook.

Today's episode opens in the war room (a.k.a. the meeting room with the broken AC). Vikram, the ever-charismatic Sales Head, walks in with his signature confidence and a coffee that looks stronger than HR's attendance policy.

Manasi, our overworked and under-caffeinated Sales Executive, is furiously working through her task list when Vikram strikes:

Vikram (cheerfully): "Manasi, as discussed in my email, we need the updated client deck by today evening."

Manasi (confused): "Which email? I don't see anything in my inbox."

Vikram (unbothered): "Hmm… check your spam maybe?"

Manasi (digging): "Spam has a tempting offer on vacuum cleaners but no sacred sales instructions."

Vikram (smiling mysteriously): "Well, I definitely sent it. Might've been a server issue. Anyway, as discussed, it's due today."

At this point, I sit silently in the corner, witnessing the art of executive gaslighting with admiration. The Phantom Email strikes again.

Manasi, now trapped in a paradox of obedience and confusion, replies with the classic corporate response: "Sure, working on it now."

She didn't see the email. It likely never existed. But in the world of *"as discussed,"* perception beats proof. The email is now legendary.

So next time your boss says *"I sent it, as discussed"*, don't argue. Just summon your inner Sherlock, nod wisely, and get started.

Because in corporate India, if you didn't receive the Phantom Email… it's probably your fault anyway.

5: The Follow-up Fallacy

In corporate India, there's a special genre of email called the **Follow-Up Email**. It arrives not with answers, but with existential questions. And at the centre of this literary masterpiece is the phrase: **"As discussed."**

The curtain rises on a quiet Tuesday morning. Sandeep, the golden child of Rajiv's supply chain empire, is sipping his third cup of tea while working on spreadsheets that seem to multiply like rabbits. Suddenly, an email pings:

Rajiv's Email Subject: *Follow-up: Final Version*

Rajiv's Message:

"As discussed in our meeting last week, please find the final version attached. Kindly proceed accordingly."

Sandeep (muttering to himself): "Meeting? What meeting? Did I astral project into this meeting and forget to take notes?"

He scrolls through his calendar. Nothing. Checks WhatsApp. No messages. Replays security footage in his mind. Still blank. The only meeting he recalls from last week was with the samosa vendor.

Sandeep (replying cautiously): "Hi Rajiv, thanks for the update. Just to reconfirm—this version includes the supplier change and the revised delivery timeline, right?"

Rajiv (immediately): "Of course! As discussed,"

The phrase "as discussed" now functions like duct tape—holding together loose ends, skipped steps, and memory gaps with sheer confidence. I, sitting across from Sandeep, see him squint at the screen like a detective staring at a cryptic clue.

This, dear reader, is the **Follow-up Fallacy** in full form. The phrase "as discussed" is used as a time-traveling anchor to suggest that something was said, agreed upon, and settled—even if it never happened.

In the world of corporate chaos, clarity is optional. But "as discussed"? Mandatory.

The
Laughing
Ledger

No one remembers when the discussion happened, but "as discussed" ensures no one questions it.

Sanket
AGARKAR

6: The 'I Already Told You' Defence

In the grand drama of corporate India, memory is not just a virtue—it's a survival skill. Because somewhere between the daily stand-up and your third coffee break, your manager will say the magical words: **"As discussed."**

It's a Wednesday. Post-lunch. The kind of sleepy hour when the only thing moving fast is time. Rajiv storms out of his cabin like a man on a mission, and spots Sandeep, who's peacefully writing a follow-up email... about a follow-up email.

Rajiv: "Sandeep, the vendor data sheet hasn't been updated. Why is it still pending? Didn't we discuss this yesterday?"

Sandeep (eyes wide, stalling): "Uh... I thought you were going to send an email about that?"

Rajiv (dramatically): "Sandeep! *As we discussed!* I clearly told you. You need to remember these things!"

At this point, I glance at Sandeep. He's gone from confident exec to confused student in a viva exam. No notes, no memory, and suddenly—he's being quizzed on something that may or may not have happened.

Rajiv walks off, triumphant. "As discussed," has once again served its purpose: it flipped the burden of proof onto Sandeep without evidence, notes, or context.

Later, over chai, Sandeep vents: "I feel like I'm in a live episode of 'KBC – Corporate Edition.' One wrong answer and I'm out."

Ah yes, the *"I Already Told You"* Defence—classic corporate move. It's verbal jiu-jitsu. With three syllables, the responsibility shifts, the accountability fades, and your fate is sealed unless you've been secretly recording all conversations.

Lesson of the day? In corporate life, if it wasn't written down—it will definitely be "as discussed."

7:   The 'Let's Not Put It in Writing' Trick

Ah, the sacred phrase— **"Let's not put it in writing."** A true hallmark of corporate survival. It's that magical clause nestled in the warm, fuzzy folds of *"As discussed."* It lives in the grey area between trust and plausible deniability.

It was a regular Tuesday, the kind that screams "nothing will happen today," until Rajiv passed by Sandeep's desk, talking like a man with a verbal handshake.

Rajiv (smoothly): "We'll get the vendor quotes finalized by tomorrow, as discussed."

Sandeep (mentally scanning memory banks): "Wait... when was this discussed? Did I black out during a Teams call?"

But by the time he tried to clarify, Rajiv had vanished—like Batman after dropping a cryptic message. No email. No meeting invite. No WhatsApp confirmation. Just the lingering echo of *"as discussed."*

Back at his desk, Sandeep stared blankly at his inbox.

Sandeep (muttering): "If it's not in writing, does it even exist? I feel like I'm working in a conspiracy thriller."

I watched the chaos unfold with my usual side-eye amusement. This wasn't a mistake. This was **The Trick.** The masterstroke. The *"Let's not put it in writing"* technique is like hiding evidence in plain sight—by never creating it in the first place.

It's the perfect corporate weapon. If the task is done, credit goes up. If not? "But we discussed it, didn't we?"

Lesson? In corporate life, if it's **not in writing**, it either **never happened**, or worse—**you were the only one who didn't remember it.**

The
Laughing
Ledger

"As discussed" emails = the ultimate weapon of mass confusion.

8: The Blame Shield

In the thrilling game of corporate dodgeball, no one throws the ball faster than a manager armed with the phrase **"As discussed."** And nowhere is this more powerful—*and terrifying*—than when something goes wrong.

This week's drama began when the dispatch to a key client missed its deadline.

Rajiv (entering like a calm storm): "Sandeep, what happened to the shipment? It was supposed to go out yesterday. As we discussed."

Sandeep (squinting like Sherlock): "Sir... we only discussed that if the rates came in by Tuesday... which they didn't."

Rajiv (now casually sipping tea): "No, no. It was all part of the plan."

I could see Sandeep's soul leave his body for a minute. He opened his laptop, dug through notes, scrolled through emails, and even opened WhatsApp—nothing. No mention. No proof. No written trail.

But the deadly combo of **Rajiv's tone + "as discussed"** meant the accountability boomerang had just hit Sandeep square in the chest.

Sandeep (muttering): "It's like a Jedi mind trick. He says it, and suddenly I believe it was discussed."

And that's the genius. "As discussed" doesn't just cover past mistakes—it **redirects the spotlight**. One moment you're managing a normal task, the next you're on trial for not remembering a conversation that never happened.

It's not just a phrase. It's a **Blame Shield.** Polished. Deflective. And completely boss-approved.

Lesson of the day: If "as discussed" enters the room, and nothing was ever documented—you might already be guilty.

9: The Silent Reprimand

Ah, the final and most *mystifying* form of "As discussed"— the **Silent Reprimand**. A corporate classic where the phrase is weaponized not to assign blame… but to stir guilt like a master chef making corporate stew.

It started innocently. A supplier had delayed raw material. A new PO wasn't processed. The usual chaos.

Sandeep (shuffling to Rajiv's desk):

"Sir… I think I missed the vendor confirmation. Was that supposed to be finalized yesterday?"

Rajiv (without looking up, typing furiously):

"As discussed, Sandeep… you were to follow up last evening. These things shouldn't be reminders."

Now let me tell you, **no actual discussion** took place. I was there. The only thing they "discussed" yesterday was the best kachori spot near the office.

Sandeep's face was a mix of panic, guilt, and spiritual awakening.

Sandeep (mumbling to himself):

"Did I miss a brain-to-brain communication? Was there a telepathic sync I skipped?"

He opened emails. Nothing. Checked WhatsApp. Nada. Even considered checking Rajiv's LinkedIn for subliminal messages.

But Rajiv had already moved on, sipping his tea like a monk who'd passed judgment.

Rajiv (calmly):

"You're one of my best, Sandeep. I shouldn't have to repeat these things."

That's when it hit. **The corporate guilt trip.**

No shouting. No all-caps emails. Just a silent stare and a three-word sentence: *"As discussed, Sandeep."*

The phrase stings more than any HR memo. It suggests failure without confirming it. You start questioning your own memory, existence, and whether you imagined the entire quarter.

And thus, "As discussed" completes its journey—not just as a communication shortcut, but as a **powerful psychological weapon.**

Sandeep didn't just walk back to his desk—he floated in corporate limbo, pondering life, responsibility, and whether telepathy should be added to his JD.

Me (observing):

Forget HR policies. "As discussed" is the true feedback system here.

99% of "as discussed" emails are written in fear of HR.

The Divine Power of "As Discussed"

Because nothing says accountability like selective memory and vague reference.

In the chaotic world of corporate survival, where KPIs shift faster than Friday dinner plans and your inbox resembles a digital black hole, one phrase stands tall as the guardian angel of the overworked employee: **"As discussed."**

Let's give it a standing ovation, shall we?

"As discussed," is the ultimate life jacket on the stormy sea of shifting priorities, forgotten deadlines, and vanishing instructions. It's the **corporate Ctrl+Z**—a quick undo button for missed follow-ups and undocumented instructions. When used right, it can deflect accountability, confuse your boss *and* your teammate, and still sound oddly professional.

Got a task you forgot?

⇒ Just say: "I assumed we'd aligned on that—as discussed."

   Was never part of the project but got pulled in suddenly?

⇒ Smile and say: "Oh yes, as discussed, I was meant to support the backend work."

   Didn't read the email chain?

⇒ Just channel your inner Zen master and whisper, "It was covered—as discussed."

It's elegant. It's subtle. It's vaguely threatening. And best of all, it's **untraceable**.

But let's not pretend it's all rainbows and samosas. When things blow up—and *they always do*—you'll find yourself on the receiving end of a cold, confident:

"Sandeep, this was clearly mentioned... as discussed."

No timestamp. No minutes of meeting. Just pure, guilt-soaked ambiguity.

This is when you start questioning your memory, your job, your existence, and whether you've been part of an imaginary discussion cult the whole time.

Still, if used wisely, "As discussed" is the **corporate invisibility cloak** that shields you from politics, prevents blame from sticking, and makes you look like you're always two steps ahead—even if you're just trying to figure out what the actual task was.

So, remember, in the eternal battlefield of meetings, mails, and mild existential panic, your best weapon isn't strategy or skill… it's confidence in saying:

"As discussed."

And if anyone challenges you?

Just smile, sip your chai, and say,

"You must've forgotten. We aligned on this… as discussed."

Corporate trainings

**CORPORATE TRAININGS:
POWERPOINT PURGATORY**

Welcome to the mystical realm of **corporate trainings**—a place where motivation meets monotony, and your path to professional growth begins with a 94-slide PDF titled **"Cybersecurity Compliance for the**

Modern Employee." Spoiler alert: Slide 53 is just a pie chart showing how many employees fall asleep by Slide 40.

In Indian corporate culture, "mandatory training" is a rite of passage. It's like the workplace's version of spiritual awakening—except instead of meditating, you're clicking "Next" on a poorly animated module while pretending to take notes.

These trainings are not just educational—they're designed to **test your patience, comprehension, and your ability to stay awake with your eyes open.** Every topic is covered: from workplace ethics, fire safety, email etiquette, to "how not to commit fraud during lunchtime." And while the content may be critical, the delivery often feels like it was created by someone who last used PowerPoint in 2003.

You don't *attend* these trainings; you *survive* them.

Somewhere between Slide 19 ("Why Diversity Matters") and Slide 44 ("Passwords: Your First Line of Defence"), your soul gently departs your body. The voiceover narrating the module has the emotional range of a dial tone, and the interactive quiz at the end—always with trick questions—makes you doubt not just your answers, but your entire life purpose.

But it's not just about clicking through. Oh no. HR tracks your progress. You'll get gentle reminders... and then more *urgent* ones.

"Hi! Just checking in. Have you completed the mandatory module on Anti-Money Laundering yet?"

No, Nikita. I haven't even completed my morning coffee.

And just when you've survived one, another one arrives. There's always another training. Always. Like a sequel nobody asked for.

Still, we attend. We endure. We click. Because in the great corporate scheme of things, completing mandatory trainings is the closest thing we have to a team-building ritual. It's not about learning—it's about bonding over the shared trauma of Slide 78.

So buckle up, dear reader. In the next few pages, we'll explore the different types of mandatory trainings, their hidden meanings, and the absurdity we've all come to accept. Because nothing screams **"professional development"** like reading HR policies in silence while pretending to care. Let the training begin.

The Laughing Ledger

"Corporate training: Learning to handle meetings that could have been emails."

1: The "Welcome Aboard" Wipeout

Ah, the first day at a new company. A fresh start. New beginnings. Dreams in your eyes, pen in your hand, and... headphones firmly planted on your ears for the mandatory **three-hour Orientation Module** that plays at the speed of tectonic plates.

You walk in expecting balloons, handshakes, or at least a warm cup of chai. Instead, HR Nikita hands you a laptop and chirps, *"This video will help you understand the company culture."*

Manasi (new joinee) adjusts her chair, clicks "Play," and stares in disbelief as a monotone voice begins:

"Welcome...to...[company name]...we...are... delighted...to... have... you..."

Manasi (after 2 minutes): "Is the culture...slow torture?"

I, sitting nearby, try to muffle my laugh as she fast-forwards slightly, only to be met with:

"Fast-forwarding...is...disabled...please...watch...in...its... entirety..."

She groans.

Ten minutes later, the video tries to define company values with footage of coworkers pretending to laugh in a staged canteen scene. One employee even high-five the air.

Manasi (whispering): "Was that...a ghost high-five?"

HR Nikita pops her head in with a bright smile. *"How's the onboarding going?"*

Manasi: "Amazing. I feel deeply connected...to the robot narrating my soul into a coma."

The highlight? At the end of the three-hour module, you're asked to rate the video.

Choices:

Very Helpful

Extremely Helpful

Life-Changing

There's no "Please help me" option.

By the time the new joinee finally finishes, they don't feel onboarded—they feel overboarded. It's not an introduction to corporate life. It's a crash course in survival with a smile.

Welcome aboard indeed.

Corporate trainings

Nothing tests your patience like watching a mandatory training video buffer at 1x speed.

2: The Compliance Jungle

Welcome to the heart of corporate training: **The Compliance Jungle**—where your survival depends on blindly clicking "Agree" faster than you can read "Company Policy on Stationery Theft."

On Day 2, you're no longer watching videos. You're navigating a labyrinth of policies written in font size 9 legalese, each one longer than a Netflix contract.

HR Nikita: *"Please complete the compliance module by EOD."*

Sandeep (already sweating): *"This is 87 policies. I didn't even read this much for my board exams."*

Each slide contains such gems as:

"Employees must ensure third-party vendor code conduct confidentiality clause under subsection 19-B of IT-Act integration compliance."

Sandeep (scrolling): "Is this compliance or an escape room?"

Dhaval (peeking over): "How's it going?"

Sandeep: *"I passed the anti-harassment module."*

Dhaval: *"Name one thing it said."*

Sandeep: *"Uhh… something about PowerPoints being non-consensual?"*

By slide 18, Sandeep's mouse has developed arthritis, and the "Next" button refuses to appear until the full 90 seconds have passed.

Manasi (from the next desk): "I tried reading the Data Privacy policy, and now I'm scared to even send a GIF."

Me, observing this live circus of frustration, sip my chai and marvel at how corporate training manages to be both mandatory and mystifying.

When you finally reach the end, a quiz awaits:

Q1: What is GDPR?

Sandeep: General Disorder of PPT Repetition?

HR Nikita: *"Please retake the quiz."*

You don't pass these modules by understanding them. You pass them by **endurance**. It's not about knowledge; it's about who can click the fastest without breaking into tears.

Corporate trainings

HR Email: "This training is for your personal and professional growth."
Reality: It's about how not to click phishing emails.

Sanket
AGARKAR

3: Cybersecurity – Click and Be Cursed

If there's one corporate training module that turns confident employees into suspicious, mouse-hovering wrecks, it's **Cybersecurity Awareness.**

You begin with a happy face, ready to click through like all other trainings. But by slide 6, the mood shifts.

"NEVER click unknown attachments. Even if it says 'Happy Diwali,' it might be ransomware in disguise."

"Hackers can spoof your manager's email. Or worse, your HR's."

Cut to: **everyone distrusting everything.**

HR Nikita: *"We've sent the new team lunch invite on email."*

Manasi: *"I'm not clicking that. I like food, but I like my data more."*

Meanwhile...

Rajiv (the boss): *"Sandeep, did you check the email I sent yesterday?"*

Sandeep (nervously): *"No. It had an attachment... and a smiley. Classic phishing move."*

Rajiv: *"It was your appraisal letter."*

Sandeep: *"I regret nothing. I'd rather stay underpaid than infected."*

Every "HR Update" now feels like a trap.

Me, sipping chai and watching chaos unfold, can't help but admire how one training made everyone treat the printer as a potential spy device and their USB drives like unexploded grenades.

Dhaval: *"I've started replying to emails with, 'Please confirm you are human.'"*

Even calendar invites get side-eyed.

Manasi: *"Why is this meeting link so long? Is it Zoom... or ZoomClone by hackers?"*

By the end of the training, the only thing employees are sure of is **paranoia**. Cybersecurity has done its job—not in teaching safety, but in ensuring no one ever opens another email without flinching.

4: The Quiz That Makes You Question Life

You've finally crawled through the 93-slide training module. You've aged spiritually. Your eyes have adjusted to stock photo lighting. You've even accepted the narrator's lifeless tone as your inner voice.

Then... the **quiz** appears.

You expected liberation. You got **judgment day.**

HR Nikita (cheerfully): "The quiz is just a formality!"

Sandeep (sweating): "So was the Titanic's safety check."

The first question is deceptively simple:

Q1: Which of the following emails is a phishing scam?

a) Free iPhone offer

b) HR policy update

c) Calendar invite from 'Zoom2.0'

d) Appraisal letter from your boss

e) All of the above

Manasi (panicked): "I chose 'All of the above'. Isn't that what they taught us?"

Vikram (rolling eyes): "You failed. Again."

Manasi: "Better paranoid than compromised."

Sandeep scored 3/10 and blamed "ambiguous corporate philosophy."

Sandeep: "They asked, 'Is clicking unknown links safe?' Who even clicks anything these days?"

Nikita: "It was true or false."

Sandeep: "I chose 'depends.'"

Meanwhile, Dhaval aced the quiz. Not because he read the module—he just guessed based on corporate cynicism.

Dhaval: "If it sounds useful or optimistic, it's a trap."

Watching this unfold from my corner desk, I realized: **the real test isn't the quiz. It's surviving the humiliation of getting it wrong in front of HR.**

By the time everyone passed, we knew one truth: in the corporate jungle, the quiz isn't about learning—it's about whether you can **outguess the system**.

Or as Rajiv later muttered, *"Mandatory training feels less like learning, more like character development."*

The Laughing Ledger

Corporate trainings

The only thing I learned in today's corporate training? How to perfectly time my bathroom breaks.

Sanket
AGARKAR

5: The Endless Feedback Loop

At the end of every excruciating training module, right after the quiz that melted your last three brain cells, comes the sacred ritual: **The Feedback Survey.**

HR Nikita (smiling way too much): "We value your feedback! It helps us improve."

Sandeep (deadpan): "Then explain why this is the same module since demonetization."

You're presented with a survey asking deep philosophical questions like:

"Did you enjoy this training?"

"How likely are you to recommend it to others?"

"Was the voiceover engaging?"

Sandeep (typing): "The voiceover had the energy of a dying fax machine."

Manasi: "I asked if we could replace the narrator with a TED Talk."

The best part? No matter how brutally honest your feedback is, **nothing changes.**

The next year, you're doing the **same** module. Same slides. Same narration. Same boredom. Only your despair has evolved.

Survey Question: "How likely are you to recommend this training to a colleague?"

Sandeep: "Can I choose negative stars?"

Dhaval: "I recommended it... as punishment for my intern."

Even Rajiv chimed in after completing the session (yes, even bosses aren't spared):

Rajiv (sarcastically): "My feedback was: please replace this with a nap."

I observe them from the corner—coffee in hand, trying not to burst out laughing as everyone passionately vents to a form no one ever reads.

And still, next year, the same module reappears like a bad sequel.

Because in corporate life, there are two things guaranteed:

Feedback will be asked.

Feedback will be ignored.

Welcome to the **circle of training life**.

The Laughing Ledger

Corporate trainings

Corporate training tip: Nod occasionally so they think you're engaged, even if your soul has left your body.

Sanket AGARKAR

6: The 'Mandatory But Flexible' Lie

In corporate life, some things are non-negotiable—like birthday cakes in the pantry and training modules labeled **"Mandatory but Flexible."**

Translation: **You have the freedom to complete it anytime... as long as "anytime" means today by 5 PM.**

HR Nikita (casually): "No pressure. It's flexible. Just try to finish it soon."

Dhaval (relieved): "Great. I'll do it over the weekend."

[4:58 PM the same day]

Nikita (on phone, with a voice like your report card just went

to your parents): "Dhaval, the system has auto-escalated your non-compliance."

Dhaval: "Escalated to who?"

Nikita: "Your boss. And possibly your soul."

Meanwhile, **Sandeep**, ever the optimist, thought he could cheat the system.

Sandeep: "I opened the training in three tabs to increase completion speed."

Nikita (raising eyebrows): "It's not popcorn. You can't multi-watch compliance."

Even **Rajiv**, the boss, wasn't spared. He got a red warning badge on the HR portal.

Rajiv (grumbling): "Why am I being chased for this? I invented compliance!"

Manasi: "Apparently, you also forgot to *comply* with it."

It's the irony Olympics: modules titled "Work-Life Balance" delivered with the urgency of a missile launch.

I stand back, watching the chaos unfold, as inboxes flood with "gentle reminders" that feel more like court summons.

In short, **"mandatory but flexible"** is a beautiful lie—like free Wi-Fi that never connects.

Because in the corporate jungle, flexibility is just pressure with good PR.

The Laughing Ledger

Corporate trainings

Training in corporate means
the trainer reads the slides,
the employees read
WhatsApp messages, and the
manager reads emails.

Sanket
AGARKAR

7: Soft Skills, Hard Times

(Training us to be better humans... one painfully awkward module at a time)

Corporate trainings on soft skills are designed to make us better listeners, empathetic communicators, and team players. Unfortunately, by the time you finish the module, you mostly just want to strangle your mouse and communicate your feelings with CAPS LOCK.

Nikita (HR, excitedly): "This week, we have a lovely course on *'Active Listening and Emotional Intelligence in the Workplace.'*"

Sandeep: "Great! Can we emotionally skip it?"

Slide 1: *"Always listen with intent and reflect back what you hear."*

Slide 2: *"Never interrupt."*

Slide 3: *"Smiling is a form of communication."*

Manasi (midway through the video): "This course on active listening is so boring."

Sandeep (scrolling Instagram): "Sorry, what did you say?"

By the time it reaches the role-play video, you're watching two animated characters have a polite conversation about staplers with all the emotional range of an old fax machine. It feels less like a lesson in empathy and more like a hostage negotiation.

Meanwhile, **Rajiv** decides to attend a live soft skills session to "lead by example." Big mistake.

Trainer: "Let's do a trust-building exercise. Everyone will fall back and their partner will catch them."

Rajiv (muttering): "I don't even trust my Outlook calendar."

Dhaval, the unintentional comic relief of every training, raises the bar.

Trainer: "What's the most important skill in communication?"

Dhaval: "Pretending to care until it's 6 PM?"

Post-training, everyone receives a certificate that says: *"You are now a certified listener."* Ironically, no one read it.

Nikita (HR): "So, how did the training go?"

Sandeep: "I felt deeply connected... to my own frustration."

Manasi: "My only emotional intelligence was in skipping to the quiz."

As I quietly observe this beautiful circus, I realize these modules do teach me something: **how to stay calm while sitting through the emotional equivalent of a blank spreadsheet.**

Because in corporate life, **soft skills don't soften the workload— they just cushion the sarcasm.**

8: The Certification You'll Never Use

(*Because nothing screams productivity like spending 3 hours learning how to save 10 minutes*)

Corporate trainings have a beautiful irony: they teach you *Time Management* by first stealing all your time.

It begins innocently.

HR Nikita (smiling): "This one's important—it's about managing your time effectively."

Sandeep (groaning): "So I'm spending *three hours* learning how not to waste time?"

Slide 1: *Plan your day ahead!*

Slide 2: *Avoid distractions.*

Slide 3: *Always prioritize urgent tasks first.*

Manasi (muttering): "If I prioritized urgent tasks first, I wouldn't be watching this module right now."

Midway through, you get a prompt: *"This video will resume after a short quiz."*

The quiz has questions like:

What is the best way to manage time?

a) Procrastinate with pride

b) Multitask till you combust

c) Watch this video again

d) Use calendars

You pick *d)*, of course. But deep inside, you feel *a)* calling your name.

Cut to Rajiv walking past the cubicles, certification in one hand and sarcasm in the other.

Rajiv: "Sandeep, you're now certified in time management! Use it well!"

Sandeep (deadpan): "I spent my entire time getting trained to manage time. Should I manage the leftover minutes of my soul now?"

Meanwhile, **Dhaval** prints his certificate and frames it—right next to his "Excel Ninja" badge and childhood participation award in lemon-and-spoon race.

Nikita: "The certificate shows commitment."

Manasi: "So does crying in the pantry."

And just like that, you're a *Time Management Pro*—with absolutely no time left to manage anything.

Welcome to corporate efficiency. Certified and confused.

The Laughing Ledger

Corporate trainings

The best part of corporate training? The five minutes before the session ends.

9: Training Roulette – Who's Next?

(*Because in corporate life, you're always one click away from another training*)

Just when you think it's over—*ding!* —a new notification slides into your inbox like an overly excited intern.

System Notification: "New course assigned: Workplace Ergonomics."

Dhaval (groaning): "My posture is already broken. What more do you want? A spine selfie?"

You've barely recovered from the trauma of the last training on *Digital Cleanliness* (yes, that's a thing) and now the LMS (Learning Management System aka "Lurking Menace Scheduler") has thrown another module at you.

Manasi: "Didn't we just finish the Emotional Intelligence training?"

Nikita (HR, chipper): "Yes! This one is different. It's about *physical intelligence!*"

Sandeep: "If I sit straight for 20 minutes, do I get a badge?"

Each time you complete one, another takes its place. It's like playing corporate Whack-a-Mole—with your sanity.

Comic Moment – During Lunch:

Rajiv walks by, tray in hand.

Rajiv: "Did you all get the new course?"

Dhaval: "Yes, and I'm training while chewing now."

Rajiv: "That's called multitasking. Add it to your resume."

The real twist? The system doesn't stop. You complete "Workplace Ergonomics" and BAM—

System Notification: *"New course assigned: Stress Management."*

Sandeep: "The only stress is managing these trainings!"

There's no escape. Even your dreams have background music narrated by a training voiceover:

"Always sit at a 90-degree angle while working..."

And just like that, you're trapped in the Training Matrix.

Welcome to the Corporate Olympics: where you don't run—*you click to survive.*

The Training Trap—Sharpening Axes & Testing Sanity

Corporate trainings are like the spinach in a child's lunchbox—**you know they're good for you, but oh boy, do they taste like punishment.**

There's no denying their *noble* purpose. Trainings are designed to sharpen your professional axe—whether it's compliance, cybersecurity, soft skills, or the lost art of sitting upright for eight hours. They're meant to **build skills, empower employees, and create a safer, smarter, more productive workplace.**

But the journey? Oh, the journey!

You begin with curiosity. By slide 12, you're mildly bored. By slide 37, your soul starts to levitate. And by slide 91, you're googling, *"Can a human die from excessive PowerPoint exposure?"*

The robotic narrators sound like they were programmed in the late '90s. The scenarios are so out-of-touch that even your coffee rolls its eyes. And the quizzes? They make you question your will to live.

Question 7: What is phishing?

Answer A: Something fishy

Answer B: Something your boss sends with an Excel attachment

Answer C: The reason you didn't click Rajiv's appraisal email

Still, in all this chaos, **trainings do matter.** They make us more aware, more informed, and occasionally, more humbler (like when we fail the "Time Management" course because we procrastinated watching it).

So, dear employee, complete the module. Earn that shiny certificate. Add it to your folder titled "Stuff HR Will Never Check Again." And remember—every time you survive a corporate training; an intern gets promoted (probably).

Because in the end, training is like corporate gym—**you'll hate every moment, but you'll thank it when the real workout begins.**

Now, back to work. As discussed,.

Zoom, Gloom and Pajamas

"In the age of remote work, only the top half of me knows it's Monday."

Remote work was once a dream. A fantasy whispered over chai breaks— "Imagine working in pajamas, no traffic, no boss breathing down your neck?" Well, corporate heard us. And in a twist of karmic revenge, they gave us *exactly* what we asked for—along with twenty Zoom calls, fourteen Slack channels, and a permanent backache from sitting like a prawn on the couch.

Welcome to the world of remote work: where your home is your office, your kitchen is your canteen, your kids are unofficial interns, and your pets attend more meetings than HR. The commute is just a 7-second sprint from the bed to the laptop, and yet, somehow, you're still late.

It all started innocently enough—"We'll just work from home for two weeks." Cut to two years later, and we've all aged ten. Corporate life evolved into virtual chaos where pajamas replaced trousers, mute buttons became weapons of survival, and virtual backgrounds hid the messy truth: that no one has it together anymore.

The problem isn't just that we've forgotten what pants feel like— it's that we've started referring to emails as "conversations" and conversations as "alignment calls." The only consistent things in this new era are spotty internet, frozen screens, and awkward pauses where you don't know whether the person is thinking or buffering.

And let's talk about the fashion revolution—where dressing up means combing your hair, and professionalism is measured by how crisp your voice sounds over Bluetooth headphones. You're expected to be camera-ready, update sheets, attend five back-to-back "catch-ups," and still magically deliver KPIs by EOD—all while your dog is barking, your kid is asking where their homework is, and someone's vacuuming in the background.

This chapter explores it all—**the unspoken comedy of working from home**, the existential dread of "You're on mute," and the eternal search for the one room in the house where Wi-Fi works and no one's shouting. It's a deep dive into the madness, multitasking, and meetings that make remote work a special kind of corporate comedy.

Put on your Zoom shirt, fix your camera angle, and pretend you're taking notes—because we're logging into the funniest chapter of corporate evolution.

1. The Camera-On Crisis

"The only cardio we do now is scrambling for shirts when someone says 'Camera on'."

There's something about the phrase *"Can everyone please turn their camera on?"* that triggers mass hysteria in corporate Zoom land. One minute, we're all peacefully muted squares with our names floating in anonymity. The next—boom—Rajiv drops the bomb.

Rajiv (firmly): "Let's turn our cameras on, shall we? I want to see everyone's lovely faces."

Sandeep (off-camera, whisper-yelling): "Oh god. Give me 30 seconds… I need to relocate from bed to desk… which are both the same thing."

Cue the chaos.

You can hear the rustling of synthetic polyester as people scramble to throw on semi-respectable shirts over *Angry Birds* pajamas. Someone's frantically adjusting their hair with a comb that hasn't been used since their last college viva. Others activate their virtual backgrounds—tropical beaches, clean minimalist offices, or suspiciously perfect bookshelves. Ironically, the ones with the messiest rooms always have the most "professional" digital backdrops. Coincidence? Corporate sorcery.

Meanwhile, I just quietly clicked on my camera. I've been sitting here all along, dressed, present, sipping chai, watching this sitcom unfold in real time. I don't say much, but oh, I observe. Like when Dhaval joined with the camera angled from his chin, giving us a surreal view of his ceiling fan. Or when Manasi tried to switch on her camera but accidentally started her beauty filter, transforming her into a blurry anime character.

The meeting begins… awkwardly.

Rajiv (smiling): "Much better. Now it feels like a team."

Everyone else (emotionally): "It feels like betrayal."

Thus begins the day—everyone pretending they're ready, while their souls remain on the mattress five feet away.

The Laughing Ledger

Employee: "What's the dress code for tomorrow's call?"

HR: "Professional on top, pajamas on the bottom!"

2. The 'I Was on Mute' Symphony

"No orchestra compares to the sound of passionate silence on mute."

Welcome to the greatest performance of the remote work era: **"The Mute Monologue."** It's delivered daily with conviction, emotion, and... absolutely no sound.

It was a regular Monday Zoom catch-up. As usual, I had my camera on, mic off, and a hot cup of chai in hand. The meeting began with updates, dashboards, and a parade of frozen screens.

And then entered **Manasi**—charged, passionate, ready to present. Her hands moved dramatically, eyes lit up with purpose, and for two glorious minutes, she delivered what I can only describe as a TED Talk on quarterly sales.

Only problem? She was on mute.

Nikita (deadpan): "Manasi, you're on mute."

Manasi (visibly crushed): "WHAT?! That was my best monologue. I even rhymed ROI with KPI!"

The silence that followed was equal parts tragic and hilarious. Some clapped out of sympathy, some unmuted just to say "Oh nooo," and I quietly took a sip of chai, nodding in appreciation. A true masterpiece... unheard.

Next, **Sandeep** jumped in confidently, only to unmute himself mid-sentence.

Sandeep: "...and so the key takeaway—wait, sorry, I was on mute. Let me start again."

Rajiv (impatient): "Why don't we all just send voice notes to ourselves at this point?"

I didn't speak. I didn't need to. My role in this digital opera was clear—I was the audience. The silent witness to mute meltdowns and accidental solo concerts.

By the end of the call, five people had been on mute mid-speech. One pretended it was their "mic issue," another claimed "Zoom lag." But deep down, we all knew the truth:

Mute is the new ghosting.

3. The Accidental Unmute Horror

"Because nothing says 'career-limiting move' like saying the quiet part out loud."

There's a moment on every Zoom call—sneaky, dangerous, and filled with dread—when someone forgets to mute... or worse, **thinks they're muted** when they're not.

Today's victim: **Sandeep**, the human caffeine machine and Rajiv's (supposed) favourite.

The meeting started like all others: 3 minutes of "Can you hear me?", 4 minutes of "Let's wait for a few more people," and 6 minutes of Rajiv pretending to be happy.

Somewhere between slide 4 and total attention collapse, Sandeep leaned back and casually muttered near his mic:

Sandeep (mumbling to himself... but not really): "Rajiv doesn't even check emails properly... dude lives in Outlook 2007."

The digital room went silent. Even the GIFs in the presentation froze from tension.

Rajiv (slowly, menacingly): "I'm right here, Sandeep."

Sandeep's face turned from caramel latte to vanilla ice cream. He blinked. Looked at the mute button. It betrayed him. Just like HR's "open-door" policy.

Sandeep (stammering): "Uh... I meant... as discussed... in the email... that you... absolutely read?"

Meanwhile, Manasi choked on her coffee. Nikita pretended to take notes. I, true to form, turned into a statue. No expressions. No reactions. Just quiet, observational panic.

The next 30 seconds felt like we were all watching a live wire being held by a wet squirrel. Rajiv didn't say a word. Just smiled and said, **"Let's take this offline."**

Which is corporate speak for *"Prepare your farewell email."*

And that, dear reader, is the horror of accidental unmute—a treacherous button that has single-handedly ruined reputations faster than late submissions ever could.

4. Background Check: Home Edition

"Because nothing screams professionalism like a pile of laundry behind your head."

Zoom backgrounds are like astrological signs—everyone has one, and they all tell a story. Except here, it's less about destiny and more about desperate damage control.

There's the **Classic Blur**—for when your house looks like it lost a fight with a tornado.

The **Fake Office Background**—complete with stock photo bookshelf and suspiciously modern décor.

7And then there's **Dhaval**—who keeps changing his background every meeting, from Hogwarts Library to Mumbai local train.

But today, the real star was **Manasi**.

As Rajiv droned on about inventory optimization (again), Dhaval squinted at his screen.

Dhaval: "Manasi, is there… a child swinging on your curtain?"

Manasi (without blinking): "Oh. That's my intern."

Rajiv: [*pauses for the first time ever*] "…Should we be paying him?"

Manasi: "He works for biscuits and screen time."

The "intern" then proceeded to rappel down the curtain using a jump rope, knocking over what appeared to be a half-built science project and a Nerf gun arsenal.

Rajiv went silent. That awkward silence where you're not sure whether to laugh or pretend it's all totally normal. Meanwhile, Manasi calmly adjusted her angle to block the chaos, and resumed taking notes.

I, of course, stayed muted. Unmoving. A digital Mona Lisa of corporate confusion.

Backgrounds on Zoom are supposed to keep distractions out. Instead, they offer an accidental peek into everyone's real life. And the result? A sitcom more relatable than any HR-mandated bonding activity.

So the next time someone asks why your background is just a blank white wall, remember—it's not minimalism. It's self-preservation.

5. Pajamas and Productivity

"Because your Zoom avatar is the only one wearing full formals."

In the age of remote work, the phrase "Dress for success" has evolved into "Dress from the waist up."

It's not laziness—it's **efficiency**. Why waste energy wearing trousers when Excel sheets don't care what fabric touches your knees?

On one particularly *motivational* Monday morning, HR Nikita decided to restore some dignity.

HR Nikita: "Team, let's maintain professional attire during calls."

Sandeep (proudly adjusting his collar): "I'm wearing a tie!"

Nikita (narrowing her eyes): "Over a Pikachu t-shirt?"

Sandeep: "Pikachu is a team player."

Meanwhile, Rajiv, ever the traditionalist, joined the call in a full blazer. Unfortunately, he stood up mid-call to yell at his dog, revealing he was also sporting neon green boxers. Nobody said a word. But screenshots were taken. Many, many screenshots.

Then there's Dhaval, who once wore sunglasses and claimed it was to reduce "blue light exposure." In truth, he hadn't slept. Or combed his hair in three days.

And me? Always present. Always muted. Top half in formal black, bottom half wrapped in a grandmother-approved quilt. My camera firmly off. I've become a legend of mystery. Rumor says I may actually be two cats in a trench coat.

This strange half-dressed existence has blurred the lines between office and bed, ambition and apathy. Productivity continues... somehow. In pajamas. With coffee cups larger than laptops.

So here we are—running corporate marathons in slippers and attending high-stakes reviews with fuzzy socks on.

Because in this new world of work-from-home, true professionalism isn't about the clothes. It's about looking awake. Mostly.

6. The Screen Freeze Strategy

"When in doubt, glitch it out."

In the golden age of remote work, no tool is more trusted than **strategic buffering.**

Deadlines? Freeze.

Tough questions? Glitch.

Random project updates you forgot to prepare for? *Network Unstable.*

It's not evasion. It's survival.

One classic morning Zoom call, Rajiv, our ever-so-committed Supply Chain Head, was in full interrogation mode.

Rajiv: "Sandeep, status on vendor payments?"

Sandeep: *Freezes mid-blink. Mouth slightly open. Cursor trembling.*

Rajiv: "Sandeep?"

Still frozen.

Rajiv (sighing): "I hate 5G."

Sandeep (suddenly back): "...And that's the update. Hope that answers it."

Rajiv (confused): "What answers what?"

I quietly muted my laughter. Sandeep had mastered the Matrix.

Then there was Manasi, who once froze at the exact moment she was about to be assigned a task. By the time her internet "recovered," the work had magically been delegated elsewhere.

Manasi (returning): "Sorry, I think I lagged. What did I miss?"

Nikita (HR, dryly): "Nothing. You dodged a bullet."

Meanwhile, Dhaval uses his camera-freeze to nap. He captures a still of himself looking attentive, uploads it as a virtual background, and vanishes for power snoozes. Genius or outlaw? Hard to say.

As for me, I sit silently. Video on. Audio off. No freezes. No drama. But if the moment ever demands—believe me—I've practiced my pixelated panic face in the mirror.

Because in the corporate jungle, freezing isn't fear. It's a weapon.

7. Meeting Fatigue & Calendar Overload

"If this is alignment, why do I feel more lost?"

There was a time when meetings had purpose. Goals. Agendas. Direction.

That time is now... fictional.

In today's world of remote work, calendars resemble overbooked flight schedules—except nothing takes off. Every hour is a "sync-up," "catch-up," "follow-up," or worse... the infamous "pre-meeting."

And so, on a grey Tuesday, as my fourth Zoom call of the day blinked to life, I found myself staring into the void—also known as Dhaval's webcam.

Dhaval (whispering): "This could've been an email."

Rajiv (ignoring him): "Okay team, this is the pre-meeting for tomorrow's pre-alignment."

Manasi: "Wait... so this isn't *the* meeting?"

Rajiv: "No, this is to align for the alignment."

Sandeep: "I feel aligned... with confusion."

I stayed quiet, camera on, nodding occasionally like a decorative bobblehead. It's a survival mechanism.

The real comedy? Nobody knows why they're here. Everyone's multitasking—one screen showing Rajiv's face, the other showing Swiggy menus, YouTube tabs, or today's Wordle.

Nikita (HR): "Let's ensure everyone is clear on action points."

Everyone (internally): *Wait, were there any?*

By evening, you've forgotten what the original meeting was about. But you've got five new invites for meetings about those meetings.

Calendar Notification: "9 AM tomorrow: Alignment on post-sync actionable."

Dhaval: "I'm aligning my resignation letter."

And me? I quietly sip coffee, my fifth of the day, wondering if I'm part of a social experiment.

Because in corporate remote life, the only thing longer than the meetings... are the pauses between "Let's circle back."

8. The Background Noise Olympics

"Because no strategy meeting is complete without a pressure cooker whistle."

Remote work has introduced us to many wonders. One of them? The unique, unpredictable soundscape of home.

In the hallowed halls of Zoom calls, where strategy and sales targets are discussed, you'll also find the unmistakable soundtrack of domestic chaos. One second, it's Rajiv trying to explain vendor reconciliations. The next—BEEP BEEP BEEP! —someone's microwave finishes its 3-minute masterpiece.

Rajiv: "Can everyone mute themselves, please? There's a weird noise."

Manasi: "That's my dog drinking water loudly."

Dhaval: "Mine was the doorbell. Or the pressure cooker. Honestly, even I don't know anymore."

Rajiv: "Sandeep, what is *that*?"

Sandeep: "My neighbour's rooster. He's also WFH."

Rajiv (defeated): "Of course he is."

As usual, I kept my mic muted and observed in silence—partly because I had nothing to add, partly because my own background had a toddler dramatically reciting nursery rhymes while hitting a xylophone with a spoon. A true musical prodigy.

The real art here isn't speaking—it's strategically muting and unmuting in 0.02 seconds like a Formula One pit stop. You must anticipate when it's your turn, unmute, sound halfway intelligent, and mute again before your parrot starts reciting your credit card number.

Nikita (HR): "Please find a quiet place for meetings."

Sandeep: "In Mumbai? During the day? Should I borrow a cave?"

The background noise Olympics is not about winning. It's about surviving—one honk, bark, whistle, and rooster crow at a time.

9. Work-Life Blur: The New Normal

"When your office is your kitchen, and your commute is 12 steps... including a detour to the fridge."

In the era of remote work, the boundary between professional and personal life has been completely erased—like a whiteboard during a brainstorm that went nowhere.

You now attend performance reviews while flipping dosas, present reports while folding laundry, and say "synergy" while brushing your teeth. Your office chair is your dining chair. Your desk is also your dressing table. And your kid's Lego brick is now your foot's worst enemy during a presentation.

Rajiv: "Let's keep work-life balance intact."

Sandeep: "But work is now in my bedroom. Life is... also in my bedroom."

Manasi: "Sorry I'm late, was stuck in traffic—"

Sandeep: "You work from home."

Manasi: "...In my hallway. The mop was blocking the way."

As always, I remained the silent presence in the call, sipping tea quietly and watching the chaos unfold like a low-budget sitcom. Someone's child was singing *Twinkle Twinkle* in the background. Someone else's cat walked across the screen, pausing perfectly in front of the camera—perhaps to present *Q4 meow-trics*.

People no longer ask "How was your weekend?" They ask "Did you actually log off?" The concept of "EOD" has been replaced by "whenever you stop feeling guilty for not replying instantly."

HR Nikita: "Remember to log out and relax after working hours."

Dhaval: "What are 'working hours' again?"

Nikita: "That depends on your boss's mood."

And that, dear reader, is the beauty and the tragedy of this blurred life—you're always available, always online, and always a little unsure whether it's Tuesday... or still Monday.

From Zoom Fatigue to Trouser Trauma

And so, dear reader, we reach the end of our virtual maze—where every day was a mix of "You're on mute," "Can you hear me now?" and desperately trying to look professional from the neck up.

The work-from-home phase was supposed to be temporary. A few weeks, they said. Just until the curve flattens, they said. Two years and six pajama collections later, we forgot what chairs with back support felt like. We evolved into hoodie-wearing, video-off ninjas who could type while lying down and nod on calls while watching Netflix on the side.

But then came the real horror story: **Return to Office**.

Rajiv: "Starting next Monday, we'll return to our hybrid model!"

Sandeep (horrified): "Hybrid? Like pants AND shoes?"

Dhaval: "Do I even remember how to swipe an ID card?"

The struggle was real. No more 30-second "commute" from bed to laptop. Now we had to deal with traffic, packed lunch boxes, actual pants, and worst of all—face-to-face small talk. No mute button. No freezing screen excuse. No toddler or pet conveniently "ending" the meeting.

Water coolers replaced WhatsApp groups. Cafeteria gossip replaced "accidentally" leaving the call early. And meetings that were once 15-minute Zoom check-ins suddenly became full-blown 2-hour conference room marathons—with no escape except pretending to go get coffee... and never returning.

Nikita (HR): "Isn't it refreshing to be back in the office?"

Manasi: "Yes. It's like prison, but with fluorescent lighting."

The transition from Zoom to Room was bumpy, weirdly nostalgic, and sometimes tear-inducing (mostly from ironing real clothes again). But hey, we survived the chaos, the confusion, and the camera-on anxiety.

Just remember—if your boss ever says, "Let's go back to how things were," they've clearly forgotten the joy of attending Monday meetings... in bed.

Appraisal Season

*"Your Hike is Directly Proportional to Your Manager's
Mood on Feedback Day."*

PERFORMANCE REVIEW

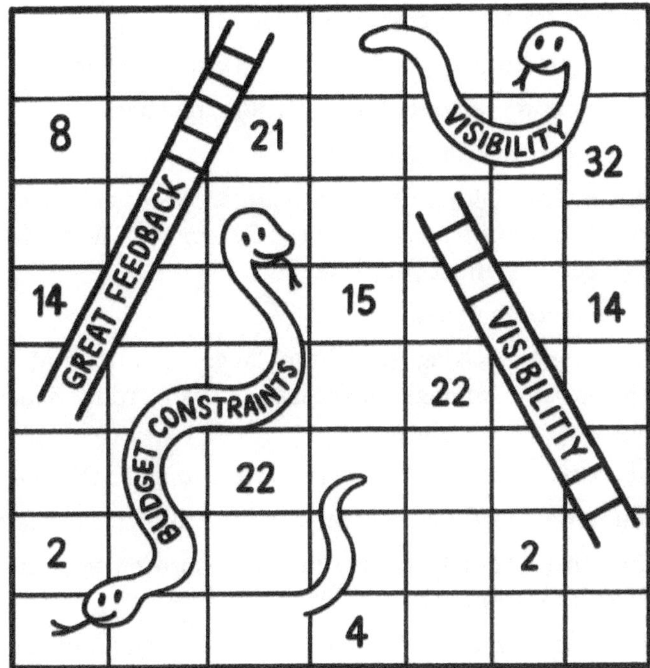

Appraisal season in the corporate jungle is like exam season in school—except the questions are vague, the grading is subjective, and no one really studied. It's the time of year when productivity screenshots are taken, half-forgotten projects are dug out from the grave, and everyone suddenly becomes a LinkedIn influencer.

Appraisal season is that magical period when employees rediscover their KPIs, managers develop selective memory, and HR starts every email with *"We appreciate your continued contributions..."*—the corporate equivalent of "Bless your heart."

And the golden rule?

Your hike is directly proportional to your manager's mood on feedback day.

That's it. Not your work, not your overtime, not even the "Above and Beyond" moment where you debugged a system crash at 11:59 PM. No. It all boils down to:

Was Rajiv in a good mood when he opened your review form?

Happy Rajiv: "You've shown great potential!"

Stressed Rajiv (post-audit): "You've not been visible enough."

Hungry Rajiv (meeting ran over lunch): "Let's circle back later."

Spoiler: Later never circles back.

The office air thickens with performance jargon. Words like *synergy*, *collaboration*, and *stakeholder alignment* fly around like confetti—none of which actually affect your hike.

And the paranoia? Unmatched.

Everyone's suddenly walking straighter, laughing louder at their manager's jokes, and adding unnecessary "Thank You!" slides in presentations.

Watercooler gossip turns into *"Did you hear Dhaval got a 20% hike?!"*

And then you remember: Dhaval organized the office cricket match.

Moral of the story? Your hike may depend more on your event-planning skills than your Excel formulas.

Meanwhile, HR pretends to be Switzerland—neutral but heavily armed with policies and unread survey data. They host town halls about "fairness in evaluation," right before releasing bell curves that squash your 4.9 into a "Meets Expectations."

Welcome to Appraisal Season—where hope floats, expectations sink, and nobody knows what *"Exceeds Expectations"* really means.

Let the circus begin.

The Laughing Ledger

"Appraisal: Where your raise is inversely proportional to your expectations."

Sanket
AGARKAR

1:   The Self-Appraisal Trap

"Rate yourself, and we'll rate how wrong you are."

Ah, the self-appraisal—corporate's most confusing ritual, where you're expected to blow your own trumpet, but not too loudly, or it might offend the gods of "humility."

You sit down to reflect on the year. You've handled vendor tantrums, survived 47 Zoom meetings that could've been emails, and even trained the intern who now reports to someone else. So, with cautious optimism, you mark yourself a 4.5/5.

Big mistake.

Enter Rajiv, the manager who sees self-confidence as a red flag.

Rajiv (to Sandeep): "Be honest. How do you rate yourself this year?"

Sandeep (beaming): "Excellent."

Rajiv (smirking): "Interesting. I was thinking 'acceptable.' Let's settle at 3.1."

Sandeep's smile falls faster than quarterly profits.

Meanwhile, Dhaval tries the opposite strategy—underrating himself.

Dhaval: "I think I'm around a 2.8. Still learning, you know."

Rajiv: "Exactly. I was going to give you a 3.5. But since you're being honest... let's keep it at 2.8."

Dhaval: *regret in HD*

Over in Vikram's camp, things aren't smoother.

Vikram: "Manasi, why did you rate yourself 4.7?"

Manasi: "Because I delivered all three projects, handled the escalation, and saved the day in Q2."

Vikram: "Right, but you forgot to CC me in one mail. Let's adjust that to 3.4."

I quietly hand in my form. No essays. No bragging. Just one line:

"Did what was needed."

Vikram looks at me. "Concise."

I nod. "Like our budgets."

The truth is, self-appraisals are like reality shows—you perform, cry a little, and in the end, someone else decides your fate. Bonus points if your manager had coffee that morning.

2: Feedback Fiasco

"Feedback is anonymous—until it's awkward."

Ah, 360° feedback season. The one time of the year when employees are asked to evaluate their bosses *anonymously*—a concept as believable as "unlimited buffet with no hidden charges."

We were told this was a safe space. HR Nikita sent out a chirpy mail:

Subject: "Your voice matters!"

Translation: "Say something... and let's see how brave you are."

Sandeep, armed with a new sense of purpose (and mild caffeine overdose), decided to pour his heart out.

Sandeep's Feedback: *"Rajiv tends to micro-manage every single task, including how many paper clips are used per requisition form."*

Fast forward two days. A storm brews in the supply chain cabin.

Rajiv (staring at the feedback sheet): "Who said I micro-manage?"

Sandeep (gulping): "...Could've been autocorrect."

Rajiv: "You typed *micro-manage*, not *microwave*, Sandeep."

Dhaval, meanwhile, tried a more subtle approach.

His feedback: *"Rajiv believes in detail-oriented leadership bordering on obsessive."*

Rajiv: "Bordering?"

Dhaval: "With due respect... bordering is still better than 'micromanaging,' no?"

On the sales side, Vikram handled feedback like a TED Talk speaker in denial.

Manasi had written: *"Sometimes, Vikram tends to schedule unnecessary meetings."*

Vikram: "Let's align on that feedback. In a meeting. Today at 7 PM."

Manasi: "And this is why I wrote it."

I, on the other hand, submitted exactly seven words:

"Leadership has room for thoughtful improvement."

Vikram read it aloud like it was Shakespeare. "Very... poetic. Was this yours?"

I shrugged. He moved on. Silence wins again.

HR Nikita insisted it was all confidential.

Rajiv: "Nikita, if this is anonymous, why is the font Comic Sans and signed 'Warm Regards, Sandeep'?"

In truth, feedback season is like a game of darts. You aim for honesty, but pray your dart doesn't boomerang. Because in corporate life, feedback may be requested... but revenge is often faster.

3: Mood Swings and Salary Slaps

"Your raise is directly proportional to the sugar content in your manager's tea."

Appraisals are theoretically based on performance. In reality, they're based on planetary alignment, your manager's breakfast experience, and the ambient room temperature during feedback.

Let's take **Rajiv**, our esteemed Head of Supply Chain. If his morning chai is too sweet, your chances of a hike evaporate faster than the milk in his kettle.

Dhaval (hopeful): "Rajiv, I've exceeded all my KPIs."

Rajiv (sniffing his tea): "Hmm. Performance is one thing, Dhaval... but consistency matters."

Dhaval: "I've been consistent for 12 months!"

Rajiv: "Exactly. Time for someone else to shine."

Translation: Rajiv's tea was too sugary and he's now bitter.

Sandeep, on the other hand, thought he cracked the code. He brought chai for Rajiv himself.

Sandeep: "Sir, kadak chai, no sugar—just like you like it."

Rajiv: "Brownnosing is not a KPI, Sandeep."

Sandeep: "Then why is it on the promotion form under 'Collaboration'?"

Across the hall, in the land of Sales, **Vikram** was having his own existential crisis—with his half-warm, half-forgotten tea.

Manasi (nervous): "Vikram, will I get a good hike?"

Vikram (sipping and frowning): "Let's not be greedy, Manasi. Happiness is a state of mind."

Manasi (under her breath): "So is unemployment."

Meanwhile, I gave my usual direct, minimalistic response:

Me: "Delivered. On time. Within budget."

Vikram: "Very concise. Very mature. Very... suspicious."

Me: *Nods silently, exits call.*

Appraisal moods are like monsoon forecasts: uncertain, unreliable, and ruinous when taken seriously. You could've saved the company from bankruptcy, but if your manager's Wi-Fi lags or they spill coffee on their shirt—*poof*, there goes your bonus.

In short, your hike isn't earned. It's survived.

Because in the corporate wild, it's not *"survival of the fittest."*

It's *"survival of the manager's mood."*

4: Bell Curve of Doom

"When performance meets statistics, emotions meet Excel."

There's a myth in corporate circles that if you work hard, meet your goals, and impress your manager, you'll be rewarded accordingly. But then comes the sinister twist in the tale: the *Bell Curve*. A shape that looks innocent in math textbooks but hits like a horror movie in performance reviews.

It begins with hope. Dhaval, the star performer—our company's own sprinting gazelle through quarterly targets—walks into his appraisal review room, back straight, achievements shining brighter than his Outlook calendar.

Then enters Nikita from HR, holding the sacred spreadsheet that determines fates.

Dhaval: "Why am I marked 'Below Expectations'?"

HR Nikita: *smiling gently like a dentist about to drill a root canal*: "We needed balance. You're... a counterweight."

Dhaval: "To what? Gravity?"

Nikita: "To Sandeep. He needed to be in 'Exceeds Expectations' this time."

Sandeep (in the hallway, eating chips): "Wait, what did I exceed?"

The curve doesn't care who worked how much. It only wants distribution. One "Excellent," some "Meets Expectations," and always—always—a sacrificial lamb in "Below."

Meanwhile, I sit in my chair like a quiet monk in the middle of a spreadsheet storm. I don't speak much in appraisals. I just write short, direct lines in the self-review:

"Delivered what was asked. Helped where needed. Survived the year."

Vikram reads it. Nods. "Succinct. Stoic. Suspiciously safe."

That's the trick. Don't get too shiny. You might attract the curve's wrath.

The Bell Curve is less a tool of evaluation and more a performance hunger game. Everyone runs, only to be judged by where they stand relative to others. It's the Olympics of disappointment.

And so ends another appraisal season—not with promotions, but with therapy memes and passive-aggressive LinkedIn posts.

Dhaval walks out, shell-shocked. Sandeep walks in, humming. Nikita adjusts her Excel filter.

And me? I quietly sip my chai, keeping my emotions off the curve—and my comments off the record.

5: The Calibration Conspiracy

"Because if you feel good about your rating, something's clearly gone wrong."

Welcome to the mysterious and mythical world of *Calibration Meetings* — the hush-hush gatherings where perfectly good appraisal ratings go to get normalized... or neutered.

It usually starts when employees, like Sandeep, finish their self-appraisals with all the confidence of someone who's saved the company from ruin (or at least remembered to send follow-up emails). He struts into the office bragging:

Sandeep: "Guys, I got a 4.9 out of 5!"

Dhaval: "How? You once forgot your own password… for a month."

Sandeep: "Rajiv said I bring 'positive energy' to the team."

Yes, Rajiv—Sandeep's manager and unofficial hype-man. But even Sandeep's sparkle can't survive the **Calibration Conspiracy**.

Behind closed doors, managers and HR gather like a secret society in a candle-lit boardroom (okay, fluorescent lights and coffee cups, but you get the vibe). Their mission? To *"ensure fairness."* Which, in corporate language, means pulling high scores down so the curve looks "balanced."

Sandeep (wide-eyed): "Rajiv, why did my score drop to 3.2?"

Rajiv (shrugging): "It's post-calibration. Think of it as... character building."

Sandeep: "It feels more like soul demolishing."

I observe silently, sipping my masala chai, wondering how calibration is always about reducing scores and never increasing them. Funny, that.

The conspiracy isn't personal. It's statistical. And because too many "Exceeds Expectations" will lead to *"talent inflation"*, the corporate system does what it must: equalize. Even if that means breaking spirits.

In the end, Sandeep's 4.9 becomes 3.2, Dhaval's 4.5 becomes 3.4, and my quiet, honest 3.5? Remains 3.5.

Low expectations = no surprises.

That's the real trick: in calibration season, aim low. It's the only score that survives intact.

The Laughing Ledger

"Corporate appreciation often comes in the form of 'Keep it up!'—without the raise."

6:   The Hike Announcement Hangover

"When your hike is just a polite reminder that inflation is real."

Hike announcement day. It's like Christmas morning for corporate employees—except instead of gifts, you're getting a PDF with numbers that should make you feel festive, but instead, feel like a punch in the gut.

It all starts with the email from HR:

Subject: *"Your Performance Review – Hike Notification."*

The moment you see it, panic sets in. You know the drill: open it with trembling hands, stare at the number, and then mentally calculate how many months of ramen and packet noodles you'll need to survive until the next one.

Manasi (excitedly): "We got a hike!"

Dhaval (checking his email, deadpan): "Mine doesn't even cover Netflix now."

Manasi (frowning): "What? You're still watching Netflix?"

Dhaval: "I have to watch something to cope with the fact that I can't afford the next season of anything."

Yes, folks, the hike email arrives, and like a bucket of cold water, it douses all your hopes. You see the percentage—4%, 5%, or, in the worst cases, 3%—and immediately begin calculating how much more you'll be paying for parking, grocery bills, and that *mildly overpriced* coffee you can't resist.

And the real kicker? Taxes. That hike? It's practically erased the moment your paycheck comes, which leaves you wondering why you even bothered to open the email in the first place.

But it's not just the low percentages that sting. It's the crushing realization that you've just been informed that you're still not close to being "market competitive." Which is HR's fancy way of saying, "You're doing great... but not enough to make us care about you as much as your salary."

As we all gather around for our "celebration," there's a strange tension in the air. Some are pretending to be thrilled; others are desperately Googling "how to live off 4% more." Meanwhile, I, the silent observer, can only sigh and hope that my coffee tastes like success... or at least, something vaguely satisfying.

The hike is over. The hangover is just beginning.

7: Promotion Illusions

"When your job title stays the same, but your responsibilities double—magic!"

Welcome to the mystical land of **Promotion Illusions**, where roles expand, expectations rise, and pay... well, stays exactly where it was. It begins innocently—with a call from your manager, filled with suspense and false hope.

Rajiv (dramatic tone): "Sandeep, we see leadership potential in you."

Sandeep (suspiciously): "And...?"

Rajiv: "You're now leading the entire procurement operations for South Asia!"

Sandeep: "That sounds... massive. What about the designation?"

Rajiv: "Same as before."

Sandeep: "The pay?"

Rajiv: "Unchanged. But think of the visibility!"

That's when you realize—it's not a promotion, it's a *mirage*. HR calls it a **"lateral enhancement"**—which is corporate for "do more with less recognition." You're still "Senior Executive," except now you're mentoring juniors, leading meetings, taking the fall for errors, and occasionally hosting training sessions—voluntarily, of course.

Sandeep: "This new role shows leadership potential?"

Rajiv: "Yes!"

Sandeep: "Without any leadership pay?"

Rajiv: "Exactly! That's what makes it potential."

Meanwhile, Manasi has been made "Project Anchor" for three major clients. No one knows what a Project Anchor does, including Manasi. But it sounds weighty. She now starts every call with, "Hi, this is Manasi, I'll be anchoring today's confusion."

I sit in these meetings, silently observing the chaos. Promotions have become puzzles, and the reward seems to be... more puzzles. Dhaval is now handling an entire product line. He keeps asking if he should update LinkedIn. HR told him, "Wait until Q3. And maybe Q4. Or never."

So yes, in the world of corporate wizardry, promotions are just cleverly disguised *workloads*. Title unchanged, salary untouched—but hey, *congratulations!*

8: The One-on-One Tango

Where vague compliments meet dead-end promises—and motivation dangles on a spreadsheet.

Ah, the legendary post-appraisal one-on-one. A carefully orchestrated performance between the employee, the manager, and sometimes, HR Nikita hiding in the calendar invite like a plot twist. The purpose? To ensure the employee doesn't rage-quit after reading the hike letter, which ironically causes more emotional damage than the actual year-long workload.

After the 4% hike revelation, the mood in the office is eerily similar to a breakup support group. Everyone's walking around with forced smiles and suppressed sobs. That's when the calendar invites hit: "1:1 Catch-up – Let's Talk Growth 😊." Growth, of course, being the most overused and under-delivered promise in corporate history.

Rajiv & Sandeep (in a Zoom room with forced eye contact)

Rajiv: "Sandeep, you're very valuable to the team."

Sandeep: "Wow, thanks. So... does that mean a better role?"

Rajiv: "No, just... valuable. Like an emotional support stapler."

Meanwhile, I sit silently in my own one-on-one with Vikram. He tells me I'm "dependable" and "the backbone of the team," which I decode as "You're too quiet to be promoted, but too useful to let go."

HR Nikita joins one of the calls mid-way

Nikita: "This conversation is part of our talent retention strategy. Please don't take it as a rejection. Think of it as... continuity."

Manasi (on mute, texting me): "Is continuity another word for 'stuck'?"

I nod back, off-camera. We all know the truth—these meetings are less about career pathing and more about emotional damage control. The message is clear: You may not rise, but you'll be *recognized*... vaguely, inconsistently, and always just enough to keep you from updating your LinkedIn.

9: Post-Appraisal PTSD

Smiling outside. Crying in Excel sheets.

Appraisals are over. Hikes are announced. Promotions (or lack thereof) are settled. And now begins the most psychologically complex phase of the corporate cycle—**Post-Appraisal PTSD**. You can spot it instantly. Everyone's walking a little slower. Smiling a little too much. Saying "Great, thanks!" with the kind of voice people use before setting their out-of-office to *permanently*.

The HR team, led by Nikita, sends out a cheerful email:

"We value your feedback. Tell us how we can make appraisals better!"

What they really mean is:

"Vent all you want. We've already locked your scores in a vault guarded by three levels of management, two policies, and a bell curve."

Manasi furiously types:

"Why is my feedback form the only place I'm allowed to lead?"

Sandeep, who once proudly declared himself "manager material," is now Googling: *"Jobs that pay in hugs and respect."*

Dhaval is busy calculating his hike on a spreadsheet. After taxes, it turns into a *reverse investment*—he owes the company emotional interest.

And me? I quietly observe it all while sipping my fourth coffee, resisting the urge to turn my resignation letter into a Mad Libs game. Vikram swings by and says, "You've taken the appraisal with such maturity!" I smile and nod. He has no idea I've been silently updating my resume under the file name *"Quarterly_ Review_Insights.xlsx."*

In the pantry, there's polite laughter and forced "it's okay" conversations. But you can almost hear the group thoughts:

"Is 2.3% even legal?"

"What exactly is a lateral enhancement and does it come with a side of fries?"

"Why is Rajiv still smiling?"

Welcome to Post-Appraisal PTSD. Where we pretend nothing happened, but deep inside, we all want to storm HR—politely, of course.

The Laughing Ledger

"Corporate hierarchy: The higher you go, the more time you spend in meetings that achieve nothing."

Sanket AGARKAR

The Great Hike Heist – Behind the Closed Doors

As appraisal letters reach inboxes and polite fake smiles light up the office floor like Diwali lamps, a secret, hilarious storm rages behind closed doors. This is the untold tale of how **4% became the magical number**, not through logic or performance metrics, but through sheer compromise, caffeine, and corporate survival instincts.

Inside the "Appraisal War Room," HR Nikita sits at the head of the table flanked by **Rajiv (Head – Supply Chain)** and **Vikram (Head – Sales)**—each holding their team's dreams in one hand and budget sheets in the other. On the screen, in all his pixelated glory, **Mr. Fillip Fouler**, the **Global Head**, joins from Switzerland. Beside him, sipping cutting chai and adjusting his shawl, is **Mr.**

Chhaganlal Katpitiya, CEO of India operations.

Nikita: "We're proposing an average 8-10% hike this year. Teams are overworked, underpaid, and emotionally drained."

Fillip (blinking): "Didn't we just give them lunch boxes last Diwali?"

Chhaganlal: "Yes, and a dry fruit box. That has *cashews*. Very premium."

Rajiv: "They delivered despite inflation, floods, and Friday town halls. A decent hike would help."

Fillip: "How much did we grow?"

Vikram (meekly): "5%... but emotionally, much more."

The room falls into a tense silence only broken by Chhaganlal's *slurrrp* of chai.

Chhaganlal: "You want to give 10% hike for 5% business growth? Who wrote this script—Karan Johar?"

Nikita (whispers to herself): "It's not about math anymore. It's about morale."

Fillip: "In Switzerland, we gave 3%. With snow."

Rajiv: "In India, we gave blood, sweat, and 43 Zoom calls."

After much back and forth, dramatic sighs, and someone googling "cost of attrition," a *grand, unanimous decision* is reached.

 Final hike: 4%.

(*But make the email font bold, so it feels more.*)

The employees expected double digits. The managers hoped for compromise. HR delivered damage control. And somewhere in the middle of chai, cheese, and chaos, *4% became history's most reluctantly celebrated number*.

The next day, a global HR email read:

"We deeply value your contributions. Here's your well-deserved reward."

Attachments:

• Appraisal Letter

- Emotional Resilience Toolkit PDF
- A blank feedback form (optional)

As always, everyone downloaded the toolkit.

Nobody opened it.

9

The Great Resignation

---

*They said "follow your passion"- so I followed
mine right out of this company.*

**One does not simply
'stay for growth.'**

There comes a time in every employee's life when the Excel sheet stops speaking to you, the coffee machine becomes your only loyal teammate, and the sound of a Slack notification triggers a mild existential crisis. Welcome to the era of *The Great Resignation*— where dreams are chased, passions are followed, and LinkedIn becomes a dating app for jobs.

The pandemic gave us many things: baking skills, an unhealthy relationship with our screens, and most importantly—perspective. Perspective that maybe, just maybe, the daily 9 AM calls weren't worth sacrificing our last few brain cells. As companies rolled out "wellness initiatives" and "motivational emails," employees began rolling out their resignations with catchy subject lines like "Moving On," "Taking the Leap," and "Not Dead, Just Resigned."

It started subtly. One person in Sales left. Then someone in Finance disappeared mid-Zoom. Before we knew it, resignation emails were more frequent than team meetings—and far more exciting. Some people left for "better opportunities," others to "pursue higher studies," and a few brave souls simply wrote: "I'm tired."

Managers panicked. HR departments started offering yoga, online therapy, and even "Fun Friday Kahoots," but it was too late. Once the Great Resignation wave hit, it spared no one. Not even Dhaval, the golden child. Not even Manasi, the dependable. And definitely not Sandeep, who was looking for an excuse since 2018.

Of course, I stayed. As always, silently observing the chaos while sipping on lukewarm tea and updating my resume on incognito.

This chapter is a tribute to those brave enough to type "Dear Sir/ Madam" one last time, hit "Send," and walk out with their heads held high (and ID cards accidentally in their pockets). What follows are the funniest, strangest, and most honest tales from the battlefield of corporate exits—where HR pretends to care, managers pretend to be shocked, and employees pretend not to dance on their way out.

Because in the end, they said, "Follow your passion." And we replied, "Will do. Effective 30 days from now."

1. The Exit Interview Olympics

A ritual where HR pretends to care, and you pretend to be honest.

Leaving a company is like breaking up politely—with paperwork. And nothing symbolizes this more than the *exit interview*—that final theatrical performance where both HR and the employee pretend to be emotionally invested in "feedback."

Enter Dhaval—star performer, people's favorite, and the newest contestant in what I call *The Exit Interview Olympics*. Facing him across the screen is HR Nikita, smiling brighter than usual, fingers poised over the keyboard like she's live-transcribing Shakespeare.

Nikita: "What made you decide to leave us, Dhaval?"

Dhaval (calmly): "Well, I realized I miss having weekends to myself. And my sanity."

Nikita: "Haha… But seriously?"

Dhaval: "Seriously."

What follows is a 30-minute polite tug-of-war where Nikita tries to mine 'constructive feedback' while Dhaval tries not to accidentally burn every bridge on his way out. It's less of a conversation and more of a passive-aggressive TED Talk.

Then comes the golden moment.

Nikita (with forced enthusiasm): "Any final feedback?"

Dhaval: "Do you want it in a poem or a PowerPoint?"

Nikita (nervous laugh): "Just… speak freely."

Dhaval (deadpan): "Roses are red, the cafeteria's bland. My growth got delayed, despite demand."

She typed something about "seeking new challenges" and "valuable contribution," while Dhaval sipped coffee like a man who had nothing left to lose.

I sat in silent admiration. Exit interviews weren't about improvement—they were corporate rituals where truth is filtered through PR language and performance appraisals are quietly judged from the sidelines.

In the end, Dhaval walked out with his final paycheck, a courtesy pen, and his dignity. Nikita filed the feedback under "To Be Reviewed Later," which in HR terms means: *Never.*

And the Exit Interview Olympics? Still going strong. Next participant: Manasi.

2. LinkedIn Goodbye Posts

Because no resignation is real until it's blessed by hashtags and stock photo emojis.

Nothing screams "I'm leaving but I still want future job offers" like the sacred LinkedIn farewell post. A ritual as important as returning the company laptop (if not more), it's the moment every exiting employee transforms into a philosopher-poet.

Dhaval had barely finished his exit interview when the LinkedIn notification popped up:

"Dhaval has shared a post."

And there it was—an emotional 17-line monologue accompanied by a grayscale photo of him staring into the distance (likely taken during a fire drill). The post read like a corporate breakup letter with lines like:

"Grateful for the learnings, the laughter, and the late-night Google Meets. Time to explore new adventures—my journey continues!"

Enter Manasi.

Having submitted her notice and completed her exit checklist (read: deleted memes from her desktop), she moved on to the most important task—crafting her LinkedIn farewell.

She stared at her screen with a deep sense of purpose (and just a pinch of drama), before typing:

"After an incredible journey filled with growth, gratitude, and great colleagues, it's time for a new chapter. On to new adventures! 🌏 #Grateful #NextChapter #KeepLearning"

Attached was a black-and-white photo of her smiling awkwardly next to a whiteboard from 2018 and a team lunch picture where three out of five people had already left the company.

The post dropped at 11:07 AM. By 11:12 AM, she had 39 likes, 8 "Best of luck!" comments, and one confused response:

"Wait, when did you join here?"

Back in the office, her manager **Vikram** scrolled through the post and muttered under his breath,

"She cried last week because the printer jammed. This better be a short adventure."

Meanwhile, I observed the show silently, sipping my chai and watching as the office WhatsApp group came alive with forwarded screenshots and ironic emojis.

Because in corporate life, your farewell isn't real until it's posted, filtered, and hashtagged.

3. The Counter-Offer Conundrum

Nothing increases your value like quitting.

It's an unwritten law of the corporate jungle: You can slog, beg, and justify a raise for years and be told, *"Budgets are tight."* But the minute you submit your resignation, *poof!* —the CFO finds a hidden treasure chest, and your manager suddenly remembers how "critical" you are to the company.

That's What Happens with Dhaval.

Tired of chasing deadlines and compliments that only came during team lunches, he did what most brave (or desperate) souls do—he resigned. Calmly. Professionally. With no drama.

And that's when the real drama began.

Rajiv, his manager, who had spent the past year assigning impossible targets and replying with "Noted" to every idea Dhaval ever pitched, suddenly transformed into a corporate Romeo.

Rajiv: "We're prepared to match the offer and even throw in a title change."

Dhaval (from a video call with a new background): "That's sweet. But I've already joined. This is my new office."

Cue dramatic silence. Followed by forced managerial optimism.

Rajiv: "Well… always welcome back. Let's stay in touch."

Dhaval: "Sure, let's sync up in my new cafeteria. They serve sushi."

Meanwhile, I sat in the corner, witnessing the classic twist in every resignation plot. A week ago, Dhaval was just another box on an Excel sheet. Today, he was a retention priority. Tomorrow, they'll find his replacement and name them "strategic hire."

Because in corporate life, appreciation always comes after the exit—and a counter-offer is just a very expensive apology.

4. Exit Season Celebrations

When strangers in your office become emotional over your departure.

There's something magically ironic about exit parties. For months—sometimes years—you roam the office corridors invisible, greeted with the occasional nod, mostly by the water cooler or in that awkward two-minute wait before Zoom meetings begin. But the moment you resign, you become Beyoncé at a farewell concert.

Suddenly, there's cake. Balloons. Emotional speeches by people who once refused to make eye contact during elevator rides.

Sandeep, ever the enthusiast (and self-appointed MC of the farewell ceremony), walks in with a cake that says *"We'll Miss You, Silent Rockstar."* The icing is misspelled. Classic.

Sandeep (grinning): "Everyone wanted to chip in for the cake."

Me (looking at 14 unfamiliar faces in the room): "I didn't know half these people existed."

Sandeep (without missing a beat): "Neither did they. But cake is cake."

What follows is a series of speeches where colleagues dig deep into their memories to fabricate anecdotes of how you "inspired the team," even if their only interaction with you was accidentally replying-all to a leave request.

"You were the backbone of the backend," says someone from Marketing.

"We'll miss your calm energy," adds someone who once confused you for IT support.

Dhaval smiled. Said a short thank-you. Everyone claps like it's a TED Talk. Even HR Nikita appears, handing over a parting gift that clearly came from the "bulk farewell mug" stock.

And just like that, in the twilight of your notice period, you become unforgettable. Not because they knew you, but because leaving is the fastest way to finally be noticed.

5. The Laptop Liberation War

Where you return company assets, but keep the emotional baggage.

Ah yes, the final showdown between HR and departing employee—*The Laptop Liberation War*. It's less of a handover and more of a hostage negotiation.

It begins with a polite email from HR Nikita:

"Dear Manasi, please ensure all assets are returned on your last working day: Laptop, charger, mouse, access card, soul."

Manasi, already halfway into her notice-period freedom, arrives at HR with the laptop in one hand, charger tangled like a bad relationship, and a mouse that's… mysteriously missing.

HR Nikita (checking checklist): "Laptop—check. Charger—check. Mouse…?"

Manasi (smiling): "I kept it. As a souvenir. It's seen things. So many right-click regrets."

HR: "Please also return your access card."

Manasi (hand dramatically over heart): "And my memories? My dignity? My unpaid leaves?"

As Nikita scans the laptop for any remaining files, a secret folder titled *"AbsolutelyNotResignationPlans"* flashes for a millisecond before vanishing into the recycle bin. Coincidence? We'll never know.

The mouse, now proudly sitting on Manasi's new home desk, becomes a silent witness to her next job's onboarding process—

while still occasionally auto-connecting to the ghost Wi-Fi network named "CorpGuest_Restricted."

Meanwhile, in the background, HR and IT are having a heated debate about whether the laptop is "intact" or "emotionally damaged."

IT guy (peeking): "Why is the keyboard sticky?"

Manasi: "Tears. Mostly during appraisals."

Eventually, the handover is declared "partially successful," Manasi signs a document she definitely didn't read, and HR smiles—knowing that she'll repeat this drama next week with someone else.

But deep down, we all know: the laptop may go back, but the trauma lives on forever.

6. The Resignation Ripple Effect

One resignation and suddenly HR is playing damage control for the entire company.

It all started with one simple email. Manasi, the quiet warrior of the office, casually dropped her resignation letter into HR Nikita's inbox. What she didn't know was that her decision was about to trigger the domino effect that would send HR spiralling into chaos.

Nikita (with the emotional range of a sad emoji): "Manasi, nooooooo... What happened?!"

Manasi (grinning cheekily): "I'm just following my passion... out of this company."

What followed was nothing short of a corporate apocalypse. Within hours, emails flooded in—more resignations, faster than HR could draft their "We'll miss you!" response templates. It was like a resignation tsunami.

Nikita, now frantically booking exit interviews, couldn't keep up. She was forced to become a full-time exit consultant instead of the office cheerleader she once was.

Nikita (pleading with Rajiv and Vikram): "We need a retention strategy! We're losing everyone!"

Rajiv (nodding sagely while sipping his lukewarm chai): "We could start by… not exhausting them with back-to-back meetings."

Vikram (in his usual deadpan tone): "Yeah, and let's stop asking them to 'wear a smile' during Zoom calls."

The "stay interviews" began immediately. Nikita would smile through the pain, asking all the right questions, while secretly checking LinkedIn for new jobs.

Nikita (writing her notes during a meeting): "So, why are you leaving?"

Employees (feeling guilty): "Well, the printers never worked…"

Nikita (nodding thoughtfully): "Uh-huh, yes, understandable. Moving on…"

As the week progressed, Nikita tried to calm the chaos by launching a "Stay Back, We Care" campaign, but even that felt like a lost cause. HR's new slogan? *"We care, but it's also the budget's fault."*

By Friday, the ripple effect had caught up with the entire company. Employees were resigning just to get free cake at their exit parties.

7. Notice Period Nomads

The strange limbo between resignation and freedom.

Ah, the notice period. A time when you're physically present but emotionally on vacation. You're still sitting at your desk, replying to emails, attending meetings, but mentally you've already packed your bags and boarded the "I'm outta here" flight.

Manasi, who had submitted her resignation a week ago, was now in full Notice Period Nomad mode. She was the living embodiment of a person who had checked out, yet still had to go through the motions of pretending to work. It was a time of strategic email deletions, subtle task delegations, and the occasional fake sprint to the printer.

Vikram (glancing at Manasi's screen): "Can you take this up?"

Manasi (glancing at him with a deadpan expression): "I've already taken off emotionally."

Vikram (sighing): "But we need this done before you leave."

Manasi (typing furiously while half-watching Netflix on mute): "Per my last day..."

Vikram, trying to hold onto whatever sliver of responsibility Manasi had left, kept piling on the work. But Manasi was as efficient as a person in a hammock on a tropical island, with a drink in one hand and a "not my problem" attitude in the other.

The real kicker? She was still attending the mandatory stand-ups and Zoom calls, all while delivering the bare minimum, contributing just enough to avoid suspicion but not enough to be useful.

Vikram (during a meeting): "Manasi, can you give us an update on the client call?"

Manasi (quickly typing on her phone): "Client's happy. I've already mentally checked out. Next?"

Vikram (rubbing his forehead): "I can feel my will to live draining."

The notice period was truly the office's version of the "middle seat" on a plane—uncomfortable, awkward, and full of people trying not to make eye contact.

8. The Great 'Rehire' Circle

"You complete the circle of corporate life... like a boomerang with a résumé."

It's been six glorious months since Dhaval left the company. He's grown, he's learned, he's bought a ring light for better Zoom lighting. Life was good—until he received a curious email from Rajiv:

Subject: *Exciting Opportunity to Reconnect!*

Translation: "We're desperate, and Rajiv finally admitted you were useful."

Rajiv wanted Dhaval back. Only now, the role had a new name:

Re-Engagement Specialist. Same work, same pay—just with a title that sounded like it required spiritual counselling certifications.

Dhaval (on call): "So... I left for growth, and now I'm being offered growth... in reverse?"

Rajiv (cheerfully): "It's a lateral comeback with upward potential for sideways impact."

Dhaval: "Did you just invent that sentence on the spot?"

Rajiv (laughing nervously): "Haha, synergy!"

The HR pitch was even more dramatic.

Nikita: "This is a unique role tailored just for you."

Dhaval: "Then why is it on LinkedIn under 'Urgently Hiring' with 48 applicants?"

Nikita: "Because... you're unique... among 48."

Despite the rebranding, nothing had changed—same chaos, same overbooked calendar invites, and same Rajiv with his "quick syncs" that lasted an hour. Except now, Dhaval's desk plant had died at his new job and he was *slightly* considering it.

But the irony wasn't lost on him.

Dhaval (in group chat): "Imagine quitting your job just to be invited back like a guest appearance on a show that cancelled you."

Sandeep: "Tell them you'll return only if Rajiv gets demoted to 'Dis-Engagement Manager.'"

Corporate life really is a cycle—first they ignore your ideas, then they fire someone who agreed with them, then they ask you to come back and implement them.

9. Finding Your Passion (Or a Less Annoying Boss)

"You didn't find your passion—just a place where the meetings end on time and people don't say 'let's circle back.'"

It's been six months since Dhaval escaped the corporate labyrinth. He now works at a unicorn startup with a smoothie bar, dog-friendly Tuesdays, and something called "Email-Free Fridays."

Meanwhile, I'm still here—head down, camera off, quietly surviving Rajiv's "strategic realignments" and HR's motivational posters.

Dhaval video-called me during my 8th meeting of the day, sipping cold brew from a mason jar that cost more than my lunch.

Dhaval: "How's the office?"

Me: "Still exists."

Dhaval: "Any new jargon?"

Me: "We now 'co-create' problems instead of solving them."

Dhaval: "Corporate poetry."

He shared how in his new company, meetings begin with mindfulness, end on time, and "circling back" is a fireable offense.

Dhaval: "Here, if a meeting has no agenda, it gets canceled."

Me: "Here, if a meeting has an agenda, it's still confusing."

He asked if I'd found my passion yet. I looked around—same desk, same Teams ping from Sandeep, same Rajiv voice saying, "Let's touch base offline."

Me: "Not yet. But I've mastered the art of appearing frozen on Zoom."

We laughed. Well, Dhaval did. I chuckled silently—then quickly got back to updating the tracker that nobody opens.

Passion, perhaps, wasn't about quitting. It was knowing your worth, staying calm in chaos... and someday forwarding your resignation with the subject: *"Following my passion (and better coffee)."*

"They said love your job, not your company. Because you never know when your company stops loving you back."

The Great Resignation wasn't just a wave—it was a full-blown tsunami of exit emails, farewell cakes, and LinkedIn posts featuring quotes from Steve Jobs and blurry group photos. From Dhaval to Manasi, half the office chairs started spinning from sudden disappearances.

Some called it "career clarity." Others just wanted a place where "flexible hours" didn't mean *working all the hours.*

One moment, you're "a valuable asset," and the next, you're being replaced by an Excel macro. That's when people started realizing that perhaps loyalty is overrated—and lunch breaks are underrated.

"Passion is not found in your company's vision slide deck. It's found in places where you don't have to CC 12 people for permission to think."

We've seen it all:

HR Nikita smiling like a resignation is a mild inconvenience.

Rajiv pretending hikes don't depend on his blood sugar level.

Vikram using the phrase "Let's nurture your role" instead of "There's no budget."

Here's the truth bomb: If your job drains you more than your gym, it's probably time to leave.

If you've started visualizing freedom every time someone says "circle back," you're already halfway out.

"Follow your passion. Or at least walk briskly away from the people who use 'synergy' in every sentence."

Yes, leaving is scary. But stagnating in an environment that treats growth like a yearly budget cut? That's scarier.

Because your job is not your identity, and your office chair is not your destiny.

So go ahead—resign, restart, rekindle your fire. Become the version of you who doesn't keep headphones on just to avoid being assigned work on Zoom.

"You were never just an employee. You were always a flight risk with potential."

And remember:

Love your job, not your company. Because when layoffs happen, even your ID card doesn't get a goodbye hug.

"Corporate Jargon Translator – Decoding the Language of Survival"

"Because 'Let's align offline' just means 'I have no idea either.'"

CORPORATE JARGON TRANSLATOR
Decoding the Language of Survival

Corporate speak is like a secret language, one that only the true survivors of endless meetings, urgent emails, and Slack messages that start with "Quick check-in?" can truly understand. If you've ever found yourself nodding in agreement while someone discusses "synergizing for greater alignment" or "leveraging core competencies," you're already well-acquainted with the enigma that is corporate jargon.

This chapter serves as your personal Rosetta Stone of survival. It's not just a glossary—it's a coping mechanism. Here, we break down the baffling phrases, the unnecessary buzzwords, and the confusing acronyms that come with every corporate interaction. With every term we decode, you'll gain a little more clarity on how to navigate the workplace labyrinth without losing your sanity.

Corporate jargon isn't just about words—it's about survival. It's about pretending you know exactly what "circling back" really means or what it means to "touch base" without actually committing to anything. If you've ever wanted to pull the curtain back and reveal the real meaning behind the corporate speak, this is the chapter that will help you do just that. Get ready to laugh, learn, and most importantly, survive.

The Laughing Ledger

Corporate trainings

The most used phrase in corporate training: 'We'll circle back to that.

Sanket
AGARKAR

1. **"Let's Circle Back"**

   Actual Meaning: I have no clue how to answer you right now.

   Usage: "Let's circle back on that in Q4."

   Translation: Let's forget this ever happened.

   "Let's circle back" is the ultimate corporate cop-out. It's the phrase that sounds like someone is taking charge and being proactive but is, in reality, just pushing the issue to an indefinite future date—usually after the next quarter, when all your hopes and dreams of resolution have likely faded.

   You've heard it in every meeting: someone asks a simple question, and suddenly the entire room shifts uncomfortably. It's time for the magic words to come out. Someone—likely a manager or director—grins and says, "Let's circle back on that," and the group nods solemnly, pretending that no one has any idea what's really going on.

What this phrase really means is that the speaker doesn't have a clue, doesn't want to deal with it right now, and will push the issue far enough down the road that by the time you circle back, you've completely forgotten what you were even talking about.

It's the perfect escape. The corporate equivalent of a "we'll get back to you." But really, it's the beginning of the end. The phrase signals a polite way to sweep the problem under the rug—until it's so far out of sight that it might as well never have existed.

The Laughing Ledger

Manager: "Let's take this offline."

Employee: "Sure, and leave it there forever."

2. **"Take This Offline"**

Actual Meaning: You just exposed something awkward in front of everyone.

Usage: "Good point, Dhaval, let's take this offline."

Translation: You're ruining my image—shut up politely.

Ah yes, the classic "Take this offline." It sounds productive, mature, even action-oriented. But beneath its calm surface lies panic, embarrassment, and a desperate attempt to protect someone's credibility—usually the person who just got caught winging it in a Zoom call.

You know it's coming the moment Dhaval asks a perfectly logical but mildly inconvenient question like, "Didn't we allocate budget for this last quarter?" Everyone freezes. Rajiv clears his throat, flashes a tight-lipped smile and says, "Great point, Dhaval, let's take this offline."

Translation: *Please stop before the CEO asks me the same thing.*

It's the corporate version of throwing a blanket over a fire—while the room is still filling with smoke.

"Let's take this offline" = "Let's bury this before legal gets involved."

"It's not a meeting until someone says, "We'll take it offline," and no one ever brings it back online."

"The only thing that goes more offline than this topic is the office printer during appraisal week."

So the next time someone offers to "take it offline," just know— you've touched a nerve. Congratulations, truth-teller.

3. **"Low-Hanging Fruit"**

Actual Meaning: Something so basic we'll pretend it's strategic.

Usage: "Let's focus on the low-hanging fruit."

Translation: Do the easy stuff and call it innovation.

"Low-hanging fruit" sounds like a clever agricultural metaphor. But in the office jungle, it's code for *"Do the bare minimum so we can make a slide deck about it later."*

Managers love it. It gives them the illusion of momentum without the burden of real progress. At Monday's strategy meeting, Rajiv enthusiastically announces, "Team, let's focus on the low-hanging fruit this quarter!" Translation: *Let's spend three weeks changing the color of the website's footer.*

Meanwhile, Sandeep—our resident overthinker—is already drawing up a 17-tab Excel sheet to organize the fruit by height and ripeness.

Manasi once created a whole campaign based on a "low-hanging fruit" only to find out it had already been plucked last quarter… by interns.

I, the quiet observer, simply nodded and quietly Googled, "How to survive corporate fruit metaphors."

Dhaval asked, "What happens when all the low-hanging fruit is gone?" Rajiv replied, "We circle back in Q4."

So yes, low-hanging fruit: the fruit salad of corporate strategy— easy, predictable, and mostly reused leftovers from last week's meeting.

4. **"Bandwidth"**

Actual Meaning: I'm mentally fried but trying to sound professional.

Usage: "I don't have the bandwidth right now."

Translation: I'd rather bathe a cat than do this.

Ah yes, "bandwidth"—corporate's polite way of saying, *"I'm done. Emotionally, spiritually, mentally… done."* It's the magical word that makes overwork sound like a network issue.

Whenever someone says, "I don't have the bandwidth," they don't mean they're busy with critical, life-altering projects. They mean they just spent 3 hours in back-to-back Zooms, haven't blinked since 10 AM, and would rather file their own taxes blindfolded than look at one more deck.

Rajiv once told Dhaval, "Can you take this up?"

Dhaval replied, "I would, but my bandwidth is buffering."

Manasi's calendar was so full, Vikram scheduled a "quick sync" with her lunchbox instead.

HR Nikita suggested a "wellness webinar to improve bandwidth." Half the team used the webinar as a nap window.

Meanwhile, I—the quiet observer—politely smiled and typed:

"Currently at bandwidth zero. Reboot scheduled post resigning."

So the next time someone says "I don't have the bandwidth," don't push them. Hand them coffee. Or cake. Or just... slowly back away.

5. "Let's Align"

Actual Meaning: I have a different opinion and want you to adopt mine.

Usage: "Let's align before we share this with Rajiv."

Translation: You're wrong. I'll fix it.

In the corporate jungle, "Let's align" is not a suggestion—it's a soft threat. It's what your colleague says when your idea is three PowerPoint slides away from being acceptable. Alignment isn't about agreement; it's about conversion. Like corporate exorcism, but with Excel sheets.

When Dhaval presented a brilliant new process, Rajiv said, "Let's align offline." By the end of it, Dhaval's idea had morphed into Rajiv's quarterly vision.

Sandeep once tried aligning with three teams. He returned looking like he'd just negotiated a peace treaty at the UN.

Manasi whispered, "Can we align on this deck?" Translation: *"I've already changed it, I'm just informing you."*

Alignment meetings are where creativity goes to die—silently, diplomatically, and in bullet points.

Meanwhile, I—the silent observer—nodded at every "Let's align," and saved both versions of the file:

"My_idea_final_final_v6.pptx"

and

"Aligned_with_everyone_but_nobody_is_happy.pptx"

In short, if someone asks to align, brace yourself. A storm of polite domination is coming.

6.   **"Strategic Synergies"**

Actual Meaning: We don't know what we're doing, but we'll do it together.

Usage: "This partnership brings strategic synergies."

Translation: Two confused teams are better than one.

Ah, *strategic synergies*—the ultimate phrase when management wants to sound visionary while merging two completely unrelated departments. Think of it as throwing spaghetti at a wall *and* adding cheese to see what sticks.

When Supply Chain and Marketing were asked to "collaborate for strategic synergy," Rajiv looked at Vikram like they were on a blind date arranged by HR.

Rajiv: "So...you sell?"

Vikram: "So...you supply?"

Meanwhile, Manasi was asked to "leverage the cross-functional energy," which she translated as "attend more meetings with fewer outcomes."

Dhaval once tried explaining a synergy chart to a vendor. The vendor left thinking we were launching a circus.

Sandeep, ever the optimist, said, "Let's give synergy a chance." Three weeks later, he was found deep in a spreadsheet muttering, "Whose idea was this?"

I—your quiet narrator—attended the synergy kick-off meeting, nodded wisely, and renamed the folder:

"Strategic Confusion - Phase 1"

Because nothing screams synergy like shared panic and synchronized chaos.

7. "Value Addition"

Actual Meaning: Something we're doing anyway, now repackaged to look intentional.

Usage: "This deck provides great value addition."

Translation: I added a slide with emojis. Appreciate me.

"Value addition" is the corporate version of putting glitter on cardboard and calling it premium packaging. It's what happens when someone renames "Monday report" as "Weekly Strategic Digest" and expects applause.

Take Sandeep's presentation: the same old pie chart, but now with jazz hands (read: animated transitions).

Rajiv, nodding: "This has tremendous value addition."

Dhaval, whispering: "He just changed the font to Comic Sans."

Once, HR Nikita emailed a company-wide update labelled *"Value-Added Insights."*

The insights? "Let's drink more water" and "Don't click suspicious links."

Truly, the wisdom of the ages.

Manasi renamed "Excel Sheet V23" to "Performance Analytics Dashboard." Suddenly, she was invited to present in front of the CEO.

I once renamed a file from "Final_PPT_LastVersion_3_FINAL_FINAL.pptx" to "Strategic Deck_Q4" and got a "Thank you for your contribution" from Vikram.

Lesson? In corporate life, it's not about what you do. It's how convincingly you label it.

And if all else fails—just add a graph and say, "This is for better stakeholder alignment."

Boom. Value added.

8. "Let Me Loop In..."

Actual Meaning: I need someone else to deal with this.

Usage: "Let me loop in Vikram from Sales."

Translation: Not my circus, not my monkeys.

"Let me loop in..." is the corporate equivalent of passing the hot potato—gracefully, and with a Cc. It's the art of forwarding responsibility like it's an Olympic relay baton.

The moment things get confusing, complex, or mildly annoying, out comes the classic:

Rajiv: "This seems like a finance issue."

Types furiously.

Rajiv: "Looping in Christina from Finance."

Boom. Problem transferred. Guilt evaporated.

One time, Dhaval asked about a technical glitch.

Sandeep replied: "Let me loop in IT."

Five minutes later, IT looped in Operations.

Operations looped in HR.

HR looped in Admin.

Admin looped in Pantry Services.

Pantry: "We only fix coffee machines."

The issue was never resolved. But everyone felt... involved.

Vikram was once looped into a thread with 42 people and just replied, "Noted." He still doesn't know what it was about.

Nikita received a mail loop so intense; Outlook begged her to stop.

Lesson? In the jungle of corporate communication, looping in is survival. When in doubt, loop it out.

9. **"As Per My Last Email..."**

Actual Meaning: You clearly didn't read my previous message, you walnut.

Usage: "As per my last email..."

Translation: Why do I even try?

This phrase is the corporate equivalent of passive-aggressive throat-clearing. It's what you write when you'd *really* like to say:

"If reading were a skill I possessed, we wouldn't be here."

It's most often used in long mail chains where someone (usually Vikram) asks the very question you answered five emails ago—with bullet points, attachments, and even a pie chart.

I: "As per my last email, the deadline is Friday." Vikram: "So… when's the deadline again?"

Comic gold.

Dhaval once sent "As per my last email…" in **bold**, **red**, and **size 16 font**. The response? "Can you please clarify?"

Manasi's version is next level: "Re-attaching for your kind perusal." Translation: *How do you still have this job?*

Sandeep tried sending the same answer *twice*, only to get looped into a meeting to "align."

In the great corporate email Olympics, "As per my last email…" is the baton of frustration—gracefully passive-aggressive, and always ignored.

Final Transmission

As we bring this linguistic safari to a close, let's take a moment to appreciate the beauty of the corporate dialect—a language where every sentence is a maze, every word has three meanings, and silence is safer than asking, "But what do you actually mean?"

Here are a few more *honourable mentions* from the Jargon Jungle:

"Actionable Insights" – We noticed something obvious and now it's in a PowerPoint.

"Double Click On That" – Let's over analyse something until it loses all meaning.

"Move the Needle" – Pretend your two-minute update caused a company-wide shift.

"Tiger Team" – A fancy term for the same five tired employees solving everything again.

"Quick Win" – Anything that looks impressive but requires minimum effort (preferably copy-paste).

"Pivot" – We failed. Let's rename it and try again.

"Circle of Influence" – Your team... or the people who don't answer your emails.

And let's not forget the all-time classics:

"Win-win," "synergize," "robust framework," "mission-critical," and the emotionally manipulative "We're all in this together."

At the last townhall, the CEO said, "Let's leverage our core competencies to create paradigm-shifting synergies."

Dhaval whispered, "So... we're still selling soap?"

I nodded. Quietly. As always.

Corporate jargon is not just a way of speaking—it's a survival strategy. A cloak of ambiguity. A full-body armour of confusion wrapped in confidence. The quicker you learn it, the faster you decode meetings, survive emails, and escape Excel-based ambushes.

But remember—true fluency lies not in speaking it, but in laughing through it.

Final Line:

In the corporate jungle, grammar is optional, but jargon is mandatory. If you can't beat it, decode it. Or just nod, smile, and wait for someone to say, "Let's Park this for now."

Exit the Drama, Enter the Wisdom

So, here we are. You've laughed at loudmouths in meetings, sighed through appraisal heartbreaks, survived the passive-aggressive "As discussed," and mentally quit your job at least five times—during this book alone.

Welcome to the end of *The Laughing Ledger*. Or, as we say in corporate: "Let's circle back to the beginning... with key learnings."

This book wasn't just a roast. It was a love letter to the madness we endure every day in the name of work. But beneath the memes, meetings, and malfunctioning projectors, there's a truth we all live by: **humans are the only resource that can convert chaos into cash flow.**

Your systems can crash. Markets can crash. Even the office AC can crash. But your people? If nurtured, trusted, and occasionally fed birthday cake, they'll deliver the kind of value that PowerPoint can't explain.

Managers, HR, and the divine Top Management—take note:

Employees don't leave companies. They leave confusion, control freaks, and "we'll evaluate this next quarter."

Respect is the new KPI. Transparency is the new tech stack.

And "retention strategy" isn't just ping-pong tables—it's acknowledgment, growth, and, occasionally, a real lunch break.

Want to retain talent?

Don't treat humans like "headcount."

Avoid phrases like "Do more with less"—it applies to Excel formulas, not living people.

Replace 2-hour meetings with 2 minutes of genuine feedback.

And above all, **stop emailing at 11 PM and calling it 'ownership.'**

Remember: The resources you buy with money depreciate. The human ones appreciate—both in value and sarcasm.

To everyone still silently working, still muting in meetings, still replying "Noted with thanks" while their soul screams "How dare you"—we see you. You're the heartbeat of this ecosystem.

And to those chasing new adventures—follow your passion. Even if your passion is simply a job that ends at 6 PM.

So, whether you're staying, resigning, bossing, or observing silently like me—may your Wi-Fi be stable, your coffee be strong, and your manager always be in a good mood during appraisal season.

Here's to happy inboxes, healthy work cultures, and successful career exits (and re-entries).

Because in this circus of spreadsheets and synergies, if we're not laughing... we're just rebooting the system and hoping HR doesn't notice.

Good luck out there. And if it gets too much—just say "Let's take this offline."

About the Author

Sanket Agarkar

15 Years. 8 Jobs. Unlimited Passive Aggression.

Sanket Agarkar is a corporate survivor who spent 15 long, laughable years navigating the wilds of eight very different (and very odd) organizations. He gave each one his all—loyalty, punctuality, and countless unread emails—before eventually leaving them with best wishes, polite farewells, and a folder full of mental memes.

Across these years, Sanket perfected the art of silent observation. He's the colleague who rarely speaks in meetings but always knows who's getting promoted, who's pretending to work, and who's secretly crying in the breakout room. He's witnessed appraisal drama, PowerPoint warfare, and that one guy who always volunteers to "summarize the discussion" and somehow never does.

The Laughing Ledger is his debut—a hilarious, heartfelt tribute to office life as we know (and suffer) it. This book is his way of handing out free therapy through punchlines, satire, and dangerously accurate reflections of everyday work culture.

When he's not writing, Sanket enjoys lukewarm chai, dodging weekend calls, and imagining a workplace where "quick sync" is illegal.

He's lived it, laughed through it, and now he's penned it—so you can laugh too.